ANARCH
AND

ANARCHY, CHURCH AND UTOPIA

Rowan Williams on Church

THEO HOBSON

DARTON·LONGMAN+TODD

First published in 2005 by
Darton, Longman and Todd Ltd
1 Spencer Court
140–142 Wandsworth High Street
London
SW18 4JJ

ISBN 0 232 52578 1

A catalogue record for this book is available from the British Library.

Designed by Sandie Boccacci
Phototypeset in 10.75/13pt Bembo
by Intype Libra Ltd
Printed and bound in Great Britain by
CPI Bath

For Tess, Martha and Hal:
my support is growing

The Church's primitive and angular separateness . . . is meant to be a protest on behalf of a unified world.

Rowan Williams, 1989

[The Church] is pretty consistently a travesty of what it is meant to be.

Rowan Williams, 1989

Living in the Christian institution isn't particularly easy. It is generally, today, an anxious, inefficient, pompous, evasive body. If you hold office in it you become more and more conscious of what it's doing to your soul. Think of what Coca-Cola does to your teeth.

Rowan Williams, 1998

CONTENTS

PREFACE

THIS IS NOT a balanced assessment of Rowan Williams' ecclesiology. It is an argument that seeks to unbalance, to reveal an
instability. This is not necessarily to discredit: Williams would
surely agree that a stable ecclesiology would be sub-Christian; like
theology in general, ecclesiology will be *on its toes* to a degree
that would shock a ballerina. This book pays a sort of homage to its
subject by means of its suspicion of his ecclesiology.

But some will feel that it is presumptuous to approach this
man with suspicion, as if claiming to stand in judgement on his
theological existence. They are right, but perhaps they forget that
theology *is* presumptuous, all of it, whether it is *ex cathedra* or *ex*
armchair. Nothing qualifies one to talk about God. There is in
theology no position to occupy that is not terribly exposed.

I am grateful to Brendan Walsh for backing this project and to
various people who have talked with me, including Graham Ward,
Richard Roberts, Christopher Morgan, Christopher Rowland,
Giles Fraser, Don Cupitt, John Milbank, Nicholas Lash, Benedict
Green and Rupert Shortt. And above all, as usual, I am grateful to
my wife Tess, without whom . . . *crikey*!

PROLOGUE: SHOW BUSINESS

H IS FIRST TASTE of a high Anglican liturgy marked him for life. It felt like an initiation into a new religion. Here was a style of worship that felt simultaneously ancient and fresh. Though still a boy, he grasped its difference from the Nonconformist piety he was used to, which now seemed strident and thin. Here, by contrast, Christianity had an aura of objectivity, universality, calm solidity.

> I was aware of a great change in the idea of religion and, to some extent, I was aware of the nature of it. For not only was the weight of the personality of the minister lifted off (and if you've never 'sat under' a minister – what a marvellous phrase and how descriptive of the oppression! – you cannot under- stand how great a relief that was), but you became impersonal yourself, the weight of your own personality was lifted too. And, though not so obviously, this was an even greater relief. For the trouble with evangelical religion as commonly under- stood is that it is too personal altogether. There is too much emphasis on the personality of the minister and too much emphasis on the personal reactions of those who are minis- tered to – too exhibitionist on the one hand and too intro- spective on the other. There is very little conception of objective, corporate praise, as of the morning stars singing together. 'He prays best,' as the hermit St Anthony said, 'who scarcely knows that he is praying,' and what applies to individ- uals applies also to congregations.[1]

Such was the foundational religious experience of Rowan Williams. More or less. For this testimony is not his but that of the artist Eric Gill, from earlier in the twentieth century. Like Gill, Williams was raised in the Nonconformist tradition and, while still a boy, turned with enthusiasm to Anglo-Catholicism. This prefer-ence is the origin of his theological, and priestly, career. The truth of Christianity, he has believed ever since, is inseparable from the ritual life of the church. This is where Christianity *happens* – in the astonishing claim made by a group of people to belong to the body of Christ on earth. Christian truth does not exist in the realm of theory, nor in the spiritual experience of the individual. It exists as it occurs, in this distinctive social event. For Williams, as for Gill, this conception of Christian truth has a very large aesthetic com-ponent. Yet 'aesthetic' is too small a word to describe the appeal of participation in an infinitely complex cultural performance, a drama that embraces heaven and earth. This religion is not a matter of dusty old laws, or of access to some unlikely supernatural realm, it is the ultimate performing art, God's show business.

Later in life Gill lost his Anglican faith, becoming an agnostic socialist. But before long he had another revelatory experience of worship, when he visited an abbey in France and experienced Gregorian chant for the first time:

> I was so moved by the chant . . . as to be almost frightened. This was not ancient architecture such as the world used to build . . . This was something alive, living, coming from the hearts and minds and bodies of living men. It was as though God were continuing the work of creation here and now and I was there to hear, to see – even almost to touch. When I first, all unprepared and innocent, heard: Deus in adjutorium . . . I knew, infallibly, that God existed and was a living God.[2]

He also knew that the Roman Catholic Church was God's author-itative representative on earth. 'If there be a God, the whole world must be ruled in his name. If there be a religion it must be a world religion, a catholicism. In so far as my religion were true it must be catholic. In so far as the Catholic religion were catholic it must be true!'; 'I saw a vision of the Holy Church ruling the world in the name of God.'[3]

Here the difference between Gill and Williams becomes apparent. Though similarly excited by the catholic ideal, Williams remains suspicious of its institutional expression – Gill's fantasy of ecclesiastical power is a good example of what he suspects. Any communal ideology that leads one to know something 'infallibly' is dangerous, he would surely say; one must apply the rigours of critical thought to the claims of the church.

But *can* one? Can one locate the essence of Christianity in 'the church', without subscribing to an authoritative institution? Catholicism with a small 'c' sounds ideal, but is it not hopelessly idealistic? Does it not rest upon an essentially abstract and unrealistic ecclesiology?

INTRODUCTION

I WANT ROWAN WILLIAMS to tell me why I ought to go to church. But he is a busy man, and we don't know each other, so I have consulted his writings. I am, I dare say, a Christian – yet one who admits to finding the whole issue of church rather tricky: I am not very convinced by any account of church I have heard. The whole issue seems swamped in muddle and evasion. No word is more elusive than 'church' – or do we mean 'Church'?[1] Are we talking about a particular institution, a family of institutions, a cultural phenomenon that eludes institutional expression, or a supernatural reality to which every expression of Christianity aspires? Is it unreasonable to seek clarity on this, to try to pin this word down?

Williams is the obvious theologian to turn to, quite apart from the fact that he currently leads the Church to which I nominally belong. Though he has not produced a systematic ecclesiology, his work has always been centred on 'church' – on the social, communal expression of Christianity. And he is the obvious theologian to turn to for another reason. He is better than the rest. Almost no one else writing theology today displays his ability to think honestly and incisively about this religion. The average theologian, alas, hides behind either the detail of his research-interest, or his chosen brand of pious cliché. Williams is surprisingly willing to face hard questions.

I want to question his understanding of the church. This seems to be traditional, orthodox, Catholic. Yet he is a very contemporary thinker, a pioneer of postmodern theology, and also a politically radical thinker. How smoothly do these ingredients mix? Does his radical postmodern traditionalism cohere? Can it sustain the actual

ANARCHY, CHURCH AND UTOPIA

institutional reality of church, or does it in fact undermine it from within?

What is meant by his 'postmodern' approach to ecclesiology? The primary point is that Williams believes that Christianity is completely and utterly cultural; it does not simply exist *in* human culture, it exists *as* human culture. Christianity is something that human beings do – a complex mass of anthropological data, or an intricate symbolic language that the believer learns to speak. The layman would be surprised to find how critical he is of 'supernatural' or 'metaphysical' accounts of Christian faith. His reputation for 'orthodoxy' rather than 'liberalism' is in a sense misleading: his theology does not reject liberalism but incorporates it, tries to move beyond it.

And Williams' form of theological postmodernism, more than most other forms, incorporates political radicalism, though 'political' is too small a word here. What is special about *this* cultural tradition is that it contains the blueprint for a uniquely peaceful form of human society. It challenges every other form of human society, and witnesses to the possibility of universal brother- and sisterhood. This is *the criterion of Christianity's truth* – what makes it meaningful to call Jesus divine (those who doubt Williams has ever said such a thing should turn straight to page 58). At the heart of his theology is the vision of the world restored to harmony, violence and division overcome – in biblical terms, 'the Kingdom of God'; in less theological terms (which of course Williams would resist), such a vision is a species of utopianism. 'The Church exists for the sake of the Kingdom of God', he insists at one point; the church is meant to be 'in love with the Kingdom', he declares elsewhere.

From this very brief sketch it should already be clear that a huge tension lurks. On the one hand, this religion is located in a set of traditional cultural practices, whose site is church. But – and it is a *massive* 'but' – such a tradition, such an institution, betrays the fullness of its own vision. The attempt to create or maintain a Christian institution has a tragically self-defeating dimension; it entails worldly authoritarianism, the erection of boundaries, the suppression of the spirit of Christ, the deferral of the Kingdom.

Because Williams is so aware of this negative dimension to church, his upholding of Catholic tradition becomes problematic. If you scratch this orthodox Catholic, you find a very serious

critic of traditional ecclesiology, a man pushing against its constraints, quarrying for some purer possibility of Christian existence.
I am therefore suggesting that Williams is more radical than he or
his defenders want to admit. His orthodox Catholicism is in a sense
only half of the story – though obviously it is the half that is
emphasised when he is elevated to high office.

My title is therefore not merely a flash overstatement.
Williams' understanding of the church really does have to reckon
with his apprehension of the Gospel as subversive of every political
and religious order, as the good news that unlimited human community has been made available through Jesus Christ. 'Anarchy' and
'utopia' are basic aspects of this vision – and it often seems that the
traditional conception of church is sandwiched awkwardly between
them.

In what follows there is an element of detective work – for the
most part this takes the unglamorous form of finding relevant
sections within rather obscure articles, and reading certain passages
very closely. For what Williams believes is not always easily accessible. Partly this is because he is an intellectual prone to obscurity, but
chiefly it is because his career has taken on a political dimension.
Since 2002 especially, he writes to conceal as well as reveal. Unlike
any other significant intellectual of our day, he cannot afford to be
too candid about his thought. It is his duty as Archbishop of
Canterbury not to speak in such a way as might alienate a section
of his flock, and so, at least sometimes, to prefer equivocation to
clarity. We are trying to pin down a thinker who wants to remain
somewhat mysterious. I have said that if you scratch this orthodox
Catholic you find an ecclesiological radical – but it is notoriously
hard to pin him down in order to scratch him!

I am not accusing Dr Williams of dishonesty, of concealing
his true opinions for the sake of the greater good, but he is
surely mindful of Christ's advice that we are to be cunning as snakes
as well as innocent as doves. We are on the trail of a very astute
theological animal.

CHAPTER ONE

SOME BACKGROUND

H IS PARENTS WERE lukewarm Presbyterians. When they moved
   to Oystermouth, a suburb of Swansea, they began to attend
the Anglican parish church, All Saints, partly at their eleven-year-
old son's request. 'What I look back on is a sense that when we
became Anglicans there was the rhythm of the Christian year, there
was more teaching about prayer and the sacraments, and a sense of
how the whole Christian enterprise hung together in an imaginative and intellectual way.'[1] Here Rowan sang in the choir, served as
altar-boy and soon became the protégé of the vicar, Eddie Hughes,
whom he remembers as 'exceptionally charismatic and saintly'. He
soon began reading widely in history, particularly Welsh history, and
theology. St David was his hero.

Worship, as we have already seen, was the context of his apprehension of Christianity's truth. The family's transition to
Anglicanism was helped by 'the discovery of a liturgical life, and
one which by present standards was quite old fashioned but in its
actual performance was tremendously engaging for everybody.'[2]
During his teenage years he acquired considerable knowledge of
high-church ritual, supplemented by visits to Llandaff Cathedral.
Like some teenagers know about football scores, he knew about
liturgical variations. 'He was an enthusiast for elaborate liturgies', a
friend recalls. 'And he took ritual very seriously, as if it really
brought you into the presence of the divine events it depicted.'
Williams has continued to emphasise this idea throughout his
career. As he put it recently, 'the memorialising that goes on in the
Lord's Supper is not us acting to bring a distant event into our
heads; it is acting in such a way that we are made contemporary

with the act of God in Jesus Christ.'[3] High church worship is often labelled 'theatrical' in a pejorative sense, as if to say it is mere show. Williams has always sought to turn this around. Why say *mere* show? For it is God condescending to show himself through the communal drama of the liturgy.

This introduces a crucial dynamic that we shall often meet again. A very 'high' conception of sacramentalism (God is 'really present' in our rituals) co-exists with a very critical, realistic, even *anthropological* approach to these rituals. They are pieces of human culture, devoid of supernatural pretensions. Yet God chooses to be knowable through these pieces of human ritual. For these rituals define and refresh the community that God, in Christ, institutes. Whether this emphasis is essentially conservative or liberal (or 'radical'?), it is strangely difficult to say.

As a teenager he began to peer beyond Anglicanism, to see how other traditions handled the mind-blowing insight that God makes himself present in worship. 'I think one of the great break-throughs for me was when I was a teenager, and the very first time I went to a Russian Orthodox liturgy, having a sense that some-thing was going on which I had absolutely no resources to absorb.'[4] He began to learn that Eastern Orthodoxy was more at ease with the primacy of worship, less hung up on metaphysical theorising and the appeasing of Reason. And this interest tied in with his excited discovery of Russian literature (what bookish teenager does not hear the word 'Dostoyevsky' without a thrill of anticipation?).

His politics and ecclesiology, which are of course inseparable, are rooted in Welsh soil. The key is perhaps his boyhood interest in the early Celtic Church. 'I was interested in the structural freedom, the institutional freedom of it. [There was] an opposition between the quite organized, hierarchical Roman Church coming over from the Continent, and the life of the local church depending quite a lot on monasteries.'[5] This independent spirit resurfaces in modern Welsh nationalism, with which Williams has always sympathised. Like the poet R. S. Thomas, he sees spiritual significance in the cultural distinctiveness of his homeland – it constitutes a critique of soulless modernity, a parable of politics purged. This intense rever-ence for place flirts with a pagan sensibility: this impression was confirmed in 2002 when he ignored Evangelicals' complaints and became a Welsh bard in an ancient druidic ceremony.

His left-wing instincts were shaped by this form of romantic national, or regional, socialism, which had been kept alive by Welsh Nonconformism. He was not attracted by communism in its Soviet form but in its ancient local form: monasticism. There was certainly a romantic, aesthetic element to this. His attraction had a certain amount in common with the neo-medievalism of the arts and crafts movement, and Catholics such as Chesterton and Belloc. Such thinkers saw the modern industrial system as promoting arid individualism, and destroying organic social life – and of course for Williams this ties in with Welsh cultural-socialism. This capacity to romanticise the pre-modern period is hugely significant for his theology. He has been quicker to see the downside of secular modernity than its massive benefits (freedom, pluralism, prosperity).

In 1968 he began studying theology at Cambridge. His obser-vance of high-church Anglicanism continued during his under-graduate years (chiefly at Little St Mary, a liturgically correct Cambridge church), yet he began considering alternatives more seriously. Rupert Shortt writes, 'His permanent adherence to Anglicanism was not settled until 1975 or 1976. Having left Nonconformity for a "larger room", he sometimes wondered whether he might not become Orthodox or Roman Catholic on similar grounds, namely that the breadth of spirituality in these traditions could make the Church of England seem parochial.'[6] Yet outwardly he was a keen Anglican, and many contemporaries assumed that he would take Anglican orders.

As one might expect of a young Anglo-Catholic, his ecclesias-tical instincts were conservative. When Rome modernised her liturgy in 1969 he was sceptical of the change, having become fond of the old forms, which Anglo-Catholicism imitated.

He exuded cleverness, and seemed to have read everything. A friend recalls that friendship with Williams was a thoroughly intel-lectual business, that he was mature beyond his years, and low on small-talk. Yet he is also remembered as witty, fun, and a good listener. His piety was never in doubt; he did not follow the usual course of undergraduate experimentation, unless you count experi-mentation with Russian Orthodox liturgy. Friends were aware that he was attracted by monasticism. Yet his piety was not other-worldly: a fellow theology student remembers that he was much more politically conscious than his peers.

There was much to be conscious of in 1968. Above all, there

was Vietnam. This was the year of the Tet offensive and the Mai Lai massacre – hundreds were being killed daily, and television showed it to the world. But critics of America had to reckon with the violence of its Cold War antagonist: the suppression of the Prague Spring proved that Communism was even less attractive. Williams was under no illusion about this: he closely followed the Soviet persecution of the Russian Orthodox Church. Other live political issues included race: the American civil rights movement had taken a more violent course after the assassination of Martin Luther King. And the issue erupted in Britain with Enoch Powell's infamous speech. In short, global politics impinged on the undergraduate as it never had before: the world, with its violence, was closer than ever – and of course it broke out on various university campuses in this year. And 'violence' now became a prominent intellectual category, thanks to writers such as Arendt and Foucault. As we shall see, Williams brings reflection on violence into the centre of theology, and particularly ecclesiology.

In the rest of this chapter we shall consider seven different strands in the formation of his conception of the Christian church.

Anglo-Catholicism

If one had to assign Williams a label, this would surely be it. But this wing of the Church is itself a very broad church, including liberal and socialist strains, as well as more obviously 'traditionalist' ones. All that this label signifies for sure is that the wearer is not an Evangelical. Williams prefers 'Catholic' to 'Anglo-Catholic', due to the latter term's association with bitter- camp rows about incense. 'I would describe myself as a Catholic Christian', he said when he became Archbishop of Canterbury, 'meaning by that someone whose Christian discipleship is shaped by belonging in a sacramental community and consciously inheriting a certain set of disciplines of prayer. It hasn't for me got anything to do with what you wear in church or anything like that.'[7] It is worth stepping back and inquiring into the nature of Anglo-Catholicism, or Anglican Catholicism if he prefers.

England's Reformation was uniquely ambiguous. Did the Church receive a new theological basis, or did it continue on its course, but now popeless? It retained bishops, or 'episcopacy', much to the dismay of the seventeenth-century Puritans: the Church's authority should not follow the Roman model, they insisted, but should be rooted in Scripture, and the action of the Spirit in the congregation. Their brief victory in the Civil War was pyrrhic. When the monarchy was restored, it was accompanied by a traditional, hierarchical form of Anglicanism. But this nationalist Catholicism became largely secularised during the eighteenth century: its theologians often echoed secular thinkers, trying to baptise their insights.

In the 1830s a group of Oxford dons launched a high church revival, soon known as the Oxford Movement (or Tractarianism). They protested that the Church was dominated by a liberal political ideology. It must reassert its intrinsic spiritual authority – and this involved reaffirming its apostolic origins, its Catholicity. The Reformation was seen as a terrible tragedy, and Protestant thought was seen as indistinguishable from the principles of the Enlightenment. Newman, the leading campaigner, asserted 'the principle of dogma' against the eroding force of liberalism. And the central dogma 'was that there was a visible Church with sacraments and rites which were the channels of invisible grace.'[8] He rooted this in the teachings of the Fathers of the early Church. For example, he learned from St Ignatius that a bishop should be seen as God's direct representative. 'I wished to act on this principle to the letter . . . I loved to act in the sight of my bishop, as if I was, as it were, in the sight of God.'[9]

To the average Anglican, such sentiments seemed papist. And of course Newman's career proved these suspicions well-founded. He converted to Rome in 1845, deciding that Anglicanism was a compromise dressed as a church. But the move meant the sacrifice of his intellectual freedom: once he had converted he was scarcely allowed to publish anything. Had Rome been more open-minded, it is likely that many theologians would have followed Newman there. But in 1878 Pius IX declared his own infallibility, and in 1898 he reaffirmed that Anglican orders were invalid.

The Oxford Movement reminded the Church of England of its theoretical dependence on Rome. An increasing section of the Church defined itself by such awareness. Because of Rome's authoritarianism, reunion was not yet possible, but it was desirable. Throughout the twentieth century this Catholic consciousness grew, and the Evangelicals' traditional position of staunch anti-popery became increasingly marginal.

After its foundational phase, Anglo-Catholicism developed liberal and socialist variants. It built upon a form of Christian socialism developed by F. D. Maurice. He had related the doctrine of the incarnation to social reality: holiness cannot be confined to the 'religious' sphere but permeates society. This idea was radicalised by a number of eccentric activist-priests. Stuart Headlam declared that the real presence of Christ was not confined to the Eucharist but was present also in the music hall and the pub. Conrad Noel saw revolutionary import in the doctrines of the incarnation and the Trinity: 'The truth that God is Comradeship is the vital meaning of the doctrine of the Trinity.'[10] He also stressed the revolutionary significance of the Mass itself, calling it the 'prelude to the New World Order in which all would be jointly produced and equally distributed.'[11] Yet such radicalism was easily accommodated by the mainstream establishment. Charles Gore popularised a milder form of Anglo-Catholic socialism that influenced figures such as William Temple, Archbishop of Canterbury during the Second World War, and one of the architects of the welfare state.

The 1930s was a fruitful time for Anglo-Catholic ecclesiology; it rediscovered the idea of the church as the body of Christ, re-animated in worship. Gregory Dix's book *The Shape of the Liturgy* was influential on Williams – he has commended its 'very comprehensive theology of Trinity and incarnation, and the restoration of human personhood and community in the Eucharist.'[12] Such themes were also developed by Michael Ramsey, who became Archbishop of Canterbury in 1961. A new closeness soon developed with Rome, principally due to the reforms undertaken by Rome. A new dialogue was launched between the two Churches, the Anglican-Roman Catholic International Commission (ARCIC).

The leadership of Michael Ramsey from 1961 to 1973 helped to keep the young Williams within the Anglican fold. Ramsey's deep interest in both Russian Orthodoxy and Roman Catholicism showed that Anglicanism was committed to catholicity in the deepest sense, and his scepticism towards establishment was also attractive. He made the Church of England seem more interested in the Gospel than in preserving its national role. Williams learned from him 'that it was possible to be a *passionate* Anglican, to see Jacob's ladder even between Lambeth and Church House.'[13]

In the light of Williams' career path, it is clear that Ramsey's style of leadership was also influential. He began a sort of kenotic

tradition in Anglican leadership that was later continued by
Runcie. By 'kenotic' I mean that it imitated the weakness and vulnerability of Christ. Because the church seeks to be faithful to Jesus
Christ, it might not resemble a strong organisation. Before his
enthronement in 1961, Ramsey said: 'It may be the will of God that
our Church should have its heart broken' – a sentiment that
Williams has repeatedly echoed.[14] We shall return to Ramsey's
ecclesiological influence on Williams later, in relation to an essay of
1995.

Theological liberalism

Of all the influences upon Williams that we are considering, this is
perhaps the most ambiguous. On the one hand, the liberal method
in theology is absolutely inextricable from the culture of twentieth-
century Anglican theology. Williams was and is part of this culture.
On the other hand, an extreme form of liberal theology came to
prominence during Williams' early career and he decisively and
influentially reacted against it.

Theological liberalism is rooted in the Enlightenment. Since
the seventeenth century, theology adapted itself to the secular-
liberal revolution that transformed the Protestant world.
Throughout the nineteenth century Protestant theology was almost
unstoppably liberal, in the sense that it tended to make theological
categories subordinate to humanistic ones; to explain Christianity
in terms of its positive human effects.

In the early twentieth century, 'liberal Protestantism' dominated English- and German-speaking theology. In the 1920s a
major reaction to this emerged: Karl Barth's theology, which we
will discuss separately. But theological liberalism continued
almost regardless. One of the most influential figures was the
New Testament scholar Rudolf Bultmann. He proposed that
the language of the New Testament had to be 'de-mythologised'
for modern consumption. What was really meant by salvation was
a new sort of human authenticity – here he drew on the philosophy of Heidegger. Another influential figure was Paul Tillich, a
German who moved to America in the 1930s. He too favoured an
'existentialist' interpretation of Christianity.

After the Second World War, liberal theologians began to draw
on the thought of Dietrich Bonhoeffer, who had been executed by

the Nazis for plotting to kill Hitler. While in prison, Bonhoeffer began to articulate a desire for a theological revolution that would do away with traditional religious forms and concepts. Christianity must become suitable for a 'humanity come of age'. Unfortunately he was highly vague about what this 'religionless Christianity' would look like, but his yearning for a new paradigm, a revolution in Christian thought and practice, has haunted theology ever since. And it haunts Williams' theology more than one might guess. One of the first books of theology he read was Bonhoeffer's *Letters and Papers from Prison* (it was lent to him by his parish vicar). Here he encountered a martyr-prophet who was exploring the secular vocation of Christianity, who criticised a reactionary faith in the authority of the church. My whole thesis is that Williams has always been uneasily aware of this challenge, conscious that it renders his traditionalism questionable.

Liberal Anglican theology lagged far behind its German counterpart. It attempted to catch up in 1963, when John Robinson, the Bishop of Woolwich, published his controversial best-seller, *Honest to God*. It attempted to inform the general read-er of some of the developments of modern theology. The idea of 'de-mythologising' was given prominence, as were the ideas of Tillich and Bonhoeffer. Williams was not a fan of *Honest to God*: he later wrote that it reduced religion to a vague matter of inner intensity and overlooked the practical, cultural context of belief.[15]

Over the next twenty years, the thesis of *Honest to God* became increasingly mainstream. It found its principal academic expression in Don Cupitt, a Cambridge colleague of Williams during the 1980s. Cupitt argued that religion must decisively abandon tradi-tional 'realist' metaphysics, and understand itself in poetic terms. Accordingly it should abandon a claim to exclusivity, and accept that it is just one human tradition among others. We shall look at Williams' response to this in Chapter Two.

It has become common in academic circles to dismiss liberal theology as sub-Christian, to charge it with throwing in the towel to secular humanism. But this is to forget the inner logic of liberal theology, archetypally expounded by Hegel. This religion develops, he said; it is involved in historical change right from the outset, when it breaks with Jewish customs. The Reformation was another divinely ordained revolution in Christianity – and the Enlighten-ment was another. In this view, Protestantism does not give in to secular humanism; it *gives rise to it*. But does that mean that we can now leave religion behind? Liberal theology sees the absoluteness and exclusivity of traditional religion as unsustainable; we need to develop a humbler, more human idea of religious 'truth'. For Williams, this results in a mere acceptance of the secular-liberal world, with its abiding alienation. Liberals should be better Hegelians and desire the overcoming of social alienation, the authentic ethical community. And perhaps the route to this is the seemingly extreme alienation of traditional religion: it at least preserves the 'otherness' of God, and subjects our comfortable secularism to judgement. We shall later see that Hegel is a crucial resource for Williams in exposing postmodernism's narcissistic tendency.

Of course, Williams is not simply opposed to liberal theology in the way that a conventional conservative is. Instead, he builds on it. If liberal theology did not exist, perhaps he would have to invent it, for it is the necessary precondition of his postmodern Anglo-Catholicism. This is evident from his social liberalism, on issues including homosexuality. He recently insisted that

> the word 'liberalism' is complex and slippery, and that, despite the angry polemic of the right, there is no single 'liberal agenda' to be written off as apostasy. But on the other side, I want to pose some questions to an ecclesial left that can collude with the conservative caricature by assuming that there is indeed a self-evident emancipatory agenda, in which all issues can be decided by appeal to a particular definition of rights.[16]

Barth

The Swiss Reformed theologian Karl Barth (1886–1968) is not an obvious influence on Williams; he seems too Protestant to be directly relevant. But this would be a misjudgement. For it's supremely Barth who forges a space for theology after liberalism. After the First World War he denounced liberal Protestantism as sub-Christian. He briefly looked upon religious socialism as more authentic, but soon rejected it. He advocated a return to the Reformers, to their passion for communicating the word of God. His early work is marked by an obsession with God's speech, and its prophetic mediation. He writes like a poet, or a philosopher–poet

SOME BACKGROUND   13

like Nietzsche, rather than a sober churchman or theologian. It is exciting stuff.

His basic agenda was to counter the influence of liberal theology. Such theology, he argued, is rooted in the thesis of Feuerbach: that theology's true meaning lies in its human value. From this follows the 'de-mythologising' tendency we have considered. For Barth, theology must stick to the Bible's insistence that God is infinitely superior to humanity, and graciously reveals himself.

It is important to note that he had nothing in common with Protestant fundamentalism, or Evangelicalism. For Barth was fully steeped in German philosophy: Hegel, Marx and Nietzsche were in his blood. He used these thinkers to sharpen his exposition of Reformation tradition. Furthermore, he was strongly opposed to theology that emphasised inner experience and personal salvation, and ignored the objectivity and universality of God's redemption. His thought entailed a very strong critique of religion as a human ideology.

His style is basic to his work: he was preternaturally confident, pugnacious, witty, cool − a sort of theological Churchill. He attained prophetic status in the 1930s when he led a campaign against the Nazi-supporting German Christians. Such complicity in evil was the natural outcome of a liberal Protestant Church, he pronounced.

Barth died in 1968, the year Williams started at Cambridge. At this time the theological world was only partly impressed by Barth's revolution, which it dubbed 'neo-orthodox'. What did Williams think? Though wary of so assertively Protestant a thinker, he was significantly influenced. Four strands of this influence may be identified. First, the criticism of religion as a human phenomenon, which takes a sharply iconoclastic form in Barth's early work. As Williams has put it recently, 'For Barth, all systems for which God is an object are unsustainable: he always speaks before we have words to answer, acts before we can locate him on some intellectual map. He is never "available", though always present.'[17] Second, Barth opposed theological liberalism in a non-reactionary way. He sought to use modern critical thought (supremely Marx and Nietzsche) as a theological resource, a means to purify the tradition. This openness to modern thought, even when it seems anti-Christian, is based in a deep confidence that what is true will be of use and should not be feared. This is basic to Williams' theological style also. Third, Barth associated the weakness of theological liberalism with its collusion in dehumanising politics. For Williams too, orthodoxy is the only truly authentic form of political existence, the surest antidote to idolatrous ideologies – by contrast, theological liberalism is deemed to collude with the innate violence of 'secularism'. Fourth, Barth developed an account of Christian existence in terms of witness, communication. The point of being a Christian is not to achieve personal salvation, or contribute to some humanistic good; it is to join in God's own self-declaration, to signify his 'Yes' to humanity. The massive importance of this theme in Williams' thought will become apparent gradually. It is fed by other streams, of course, but Barth's influence should not be discounted.

Williams' divergence from Barth is also illuminating. His principal criticism is that Barth's theology is too abstract – it does not adequately admit the cultural and corporate character of God's self-communication. It over-emphasises the verbal dimension of revelation, as if God may be understood in terms of an authoritative voice that hovers over mundane reality and is individually appropriated.

MacKinnon

One of Barth's few champions within English theology was Williams' principal teacher, Donald MacKinnon, a Scottish philosopher of religion. He was an intense, eccentric, romantic, and rather scary figure. During the war he had taught Iris Murdoch at Oxford, and they had some sort of weird Platonic relationship which turned sour. Another former pupil speaks of his dangerously strong charisma, his ability to terrify adversaries.

He has been called 'by far the most influential British theologian of the twentieth century, not on account of what he wrote but in view of the impact he had on those who attended his lectures.'[18] He was awkwardly loyal to the Episcopal (Scottish Anglican) Church, deeply critical of the Church of England's establishment: a sort of Barthian Anglo-Catholic, perhaps. 'Donald was suspicious of ecclesiasticism', a former pupil recounts; 'as a Scottish Episcopalian, married to a Presbyterian, he had a thorough contempt for the Church of England – and an impatience with bureaucracy wherever you find it in religion.'

He was critical of many liberal trends, especially Bultmann's attempt to translate the Gospel into Heideggerian existentialism: 'if he makes what he is translating intelligible, he does so at the cost of making it repellent.'[19] He felt that much modern theology, and thought in general, lacked a sense of the tragic. His interest in the tragic was influenced by his close friend George Steiner.

He held that the contemporary theologian's task was 'primarily critical', and his attitude to the church was particularly critical. He saw it as simultaneously a 'continual tragedy of frustrated achievement' *and* the Body of Christ.[20] But it was the former aspect he more readily expanded upon. He was haunted by the sense that the church cannot be what it is called to be – what one critic calls 'ecclesiological impossibilism'.[21] MacKinnon said:

> It may well be that the Churches have all in one way or another failed, either by accepting uncritically the attitudes and standards of the society around them, or of certain strata within it, or else by a kind of half deliberate aversion from the problems raised . . . by means of their own involvement with the power-structures around them.[22]

He occasionally displayed something of Bonhoeffer's yearning for a new Christian paradigm, beyond old-fashioned church-based religion; a sense that the contemporary church was cursed with a failure to perceive its own failure and transform itself. In the very year that Williams met him he gave a celebrated, passionate lecture in which he criticised 'ecclesiological fundamentalism'.[23] As we shall see, Williams incorporated this sense of the church's tragic failure into his Catholicism – it is largely this that keeps it on its toes to a remarkable degree.

In an essay on MacKinnon's thought from 1989, Williams questions whether the concept of the tragic is too passive:

> The Christian commitment is to a world of reconstructed relationships, not to a venture merely of 'reading' or 'rereading' the world . . . And if – as MacKinnon many times insists – divine solidarity is a shocking and unmerciful judgement upon human and specially ecclesiastical power relations, what does this judgement change, other than ways of seeing and speaking? How shall we avoid being left with moralistic recommendations to abjure earthly power?[24]

The missing link, he suggests, is a theology of the Spirit 'as that which forms or sustains the new world of perception through the constant recreation of the Church as it is judged by its foundational charter in the paschal event.' This is a useful little sketch of Williams' agenda: he wants to develop a theology that is affirmative, practically committed to the social body, and yet no less critically astute than the thought of his teacher.

Eastern Orthodoxy

This is the most distinctive of the various influences on Williams, the only one that a bright Anglican theologian might have avoided. As we have seen, he developed an interest in Orthodox worship as a teenager: at Cambridge he began to investigate Russian Orthodoxy's modern history, which became the subject of his postgraduate research.

Until recently, Orthodoxy was more or less ignored by Western theologians. Yet it can claim to be the original church, for it was Rome that broke away from the East. The full break came in 1054, but Rome had been semi-detached ever since the barbarian invasions of the fifth century, when the papacy began to act as a pseudo-imperial focus for the kingdoms of the West.

The Orthodox Church has always been a federation of local churches, lacking the centralisation of Rome, and, at least in theory, its sharp division between clergy and laity. And its Greek origins gave it a richer intellectual foundation. Byzantium has an image as a sort of university-city, in which every market-trader cared about the finer points of Trinitarian doctrine, and saw worship as a natural part of cultural expression. This organic picture (which has echoes of Hegel's idealisation of ancient Greek religious culture) appealed to Williams; he began to study its chief theorist, Maximus the Great.

In 1453 Constantinople fell to the Turks, and Orthodoxy's political centre moved to Russia, though Constantinople remained theoretically central – its patriarch is still called 'ecumenical' (universal). But Russia now felt herself the inheritor of an imperial destiny – 'the third Rome'.

For centuries, Russian Orthodox theology was cut off from the intellectual and theological revolutions of the West. During the nineteenth century, however, contact massively increased – and

educated Russians demanded the liberalisation of church and state.
But the Russian political system was nowhere near ready to accom-
modate such thought. It was still feudal. Instead of a liberal
revolution, it had a monastic revival.

There are different reactions to this situation in Russia's two
greatest nineteenth-century novelists, Tolstoy and Dostoyevsky. In
the latter half of the nineteenth century Tolstoy decided that the
church was a betrayal of Christianity. Authentic Christianity is the
religion of Jesus, interpreted as a non-violent socialist movement.
Ecclesiastical dogma and ritual stands in the way of the Kingdom
of God's realisation. Such ideas had surfaced for centuries in
Europe, but Russia had no real tradition of progressive Christian
thought: the Russian Church had experienced neither the
Reformation nor the Enlightenment. Tolstoy was trying to import
both, rather suddenly.

Dostoyevsky was a more orthodox Orthodox. Despite advocating political reform, he was sympathetic to the Church as a
guardian of Russia's spiritual character. His novels have an icono-
graphic character, in their intense portraits of religious passion. In
The Idiot he confronts the reader with a type of Christ. It is a rather
passive, emasculated version: a pale sufferer. In *The Brothers
Karamazov* he depicts a *startsi*, or monk-guru, Zosima. And this
novel features the famous parable of the Grand Inquisitor. This
story seems, at first, to side with Tolstoy and call the church the
betrayal of the Gospel. But in the end the Jesus figure seems to bless
the church that distorts his Gospel, as if he wills to be mis-
represented by a powerful institution. Incidentally, Williams has
identified Dostoyevsky as his favourite novelist.

Nineteenth-century Russian Orthodox theology absorbed
Hegelian idealism, and domesticated it. Soloviev (1853–1900) used
such thought to reassert the Orthodox account of *sobornost*
(catholicity), which entails a conception of the innate divinity of
authentic human society. As Williams puts it:

> The Orthodox Church does not operate by external and
> legalistic systems of authority, as does the Roman commun-
> ion, nor does it countenance the individualism of the
> Protestant; it is therefore uniquely qualified to be the bearer of
> the promise of 'sophianic' humanity . . . of 'divine humanity'
> (or 'Godmanhood' as it is often rendered).[25]

In the early twentieth century the three major figures were Bulgakov (1871–1944), Lossky (1903–58) and Florovsky (1893–1979). Bulgakov, ordained as the Russian Revolution began, was a doctrinal traditionalist whose ecclesiology emerged from close engagement with political thought. Williams comments:

> [Bulgakov] sketches how theology must sail between the Scylla of social utopianism, the Church identifying itself with a confident progressivism, and the Charybdis of clericalism, the Church seeking to control the social process. What is needed is for the Church to be what it is meant to be, a living model of renewed social relationships depending upon renewed relationship with God.[26]

Lossky, the subject of Williams' doctoral thesis, had sought to root ecclesiology in patristic tradition. As Williams puts it:

> 'Tradition' in the Church is not just a process of narrowly doctrinal transmission, but the *whole* of the Spirit's ecclesial work . . . And catholicity . . . is the capacity in each believer and each congregation to receive and live the fullness of God's gifts.[27]

Florovsky portrayed history in a positive light:

> Christ demonstrates supremely what historical action is, the freedom for communion with God and man . . . The saved community is a creative community, a community of worship, ascetic self-giving, prophecy and active compassion, in which the bondage of isolation is conquered.[28]

Orthodoxy is seen by Williams as the Christian tradition least tainted by modernism, rationalism, individualism. It preserves a sense that salvation is intrinsically social. It also has an inbuilt respect for tradition; it consistently attempts to 'pursue a theology of the historical *mediation* of revelation, a theology of tradition. For many students of the field, this remains one of the most abidingly interesting and fruitful contributions of the Orthodox vision in contemporary theological discussion.'[29] Yet this respect for tradition seems less closely associated with institutional authoritarianism than in the West – and here the Anglican can directly identify with the Orthodox. Yet Orthodoxy can claim to be rooted in an older, purer theology of catholicity – that of the Greek Fathers. Williams found here a tradition that simultaneously affirmed God and humanity; it is best summed up in Irenaeus's statement: 'The glory of God is the human being fully alive; the life of a human being is the vision of God.' 'When I first came across that,' Williams has recently recalled, 'it stood out for me in capital letters.'[30] Related to this is the idea that, through worshipping God, Christians not only become holy; they participate so fully in God that they become *deified*.

Russian Orthodoxy's links with the early Church were not just a matter of ancient history:

> In the years between the two World Wars the Christians of Russia underwent sufferings which in extent and in cruelty equalled anything endured by the early Christians ... Cleansed of worldly elements, freed from the burden of insincere members who had merely conformed outwardly for social reasons, purified as by fire, the true Orthodox believers gathered themselves together and resisted with heroism and humility.[31]

This is obviously a far cry from the political situation of Anglicanism.

Williams has very often used Orthodoxy as a foil for the deficiencies of Western, particularly English, religion. Above all, it shows that the essence of Christianity is not some abstract theory but a distinctive way of life, an actual social movement. We need to re-imagine it in such terms. That does not mean he wants Anglicanism to imitate Orthodoxy – impossible due to the far greater political and social liberalism that the Church of England takes for granted. It is more a matter of seeing Orthodoxy as a sort of parable that might point us to a *new* conceptualisation of the church as a Spirit-filled cultural phenomenon.

A crucial aspect of this vision is the idea of manifestation, or 'epiphany': the church does not seek to control ideas or behaviour but seeks to *show* us God in its ritual and corporate life. Ritual is the dramatic concentration of this. For example, in an interview of 1999 Williams observes that 'the western Church has often been very prosaic and boring about the resurrection.'[32] A Russian Orthodox Easter liturgy is impressive, exciting, and fully involving of the participant:

> I think it is in that kind of environment that you would get to see what might be meant by calling the resurrection the

environment in which you live. My most vivid memory is of watching somebody running through the dense crowd on Easter Eve of Holy Saturday taking the Holy Fire on the Sabbath dawn to one of the bishops sitting on the stairs, and watching that light stream through the crowd and the whole place going on fire.[33]

In 2003, now Archbishop of Canterbury, he made a similar point. The Churches need to recapture a sense of joy, wonder and excitement – they should learn from Orthodoxy, which sees the Eucharist as 'life, light and fire. It all feels rather different from a little piece of bread.'

At root the attraction may be seen as a desire for Christianity to *feel real*. Another Anglican theologian with an interest in Russian Orthodoxy explains that, due to the Russian Church's history, and the country's continuing poverty, its liturgy has a practical urgency unknown in the West. 'When the congregation says "God save us", they are really asking God to save them.'

Roman Catholicism

When Williams was a teenager, the Roman Catholic Church tried to reinvent itself. Its modern history had been unambiguously reactionary. In the mid twentieth century, this slowly began to change.

In the 1940s a coherent reforming movement emerged; it became known as *nouvelle theologie*. Its leading figure was the Jesuit theologian Henri de Lubac. He developed an ecclesiology that moved somewhat away from the traditional, hierarchical conception of the institutional body headed by the pope, and emphasised the Eucharist as the site of the body's realisation, and the role of the local, lay congregation. This helped to inspire the Second Vatican Council, begun in 1962. The Council's most important document, *Lumen Gentium* ('the light of the world') gave Catholic ecclesiology an unprecedentedly democratic feel, and redefined the church as 'the sacrament of salvation for the world'. In 1965 an English Catholic writer summed up the changes afoot: 'The old image of the Church as a beleaguered citadel, so dear to generations of Catholics, is being replaced by the more authentic one of the Church as God's People, continuing the work of Redemption amongst mankind.'[34] But in practice the new model co-existed with the old one: the Church did not renounce its hierarchical structures and exclusivist thinking.

Williams was influenced by the Roman Catholic reformers, but especially by Hans Urs von Balthasar, who had been a member of the reformist school, but turned against it after Vatican II. He had been significantly influenced by Barth; his own work was similarly ambitious and Germanic, and similarly insistent on God's priority to humanity. Williams was also drawn to his concern with the aesthetic, and to his 'vivid awareness of the tragic quality of human existence – the hellishness of humanity and God's involvement in it.'[35] But perhaps above all Williams was drawn to a pathos of magisterial traditionalism, summed up in the judgement that modern theological trends 'lighten the ballast of what is Christian'.

It was a short book of von Balthasar's called *Engagement with God* that Williams found particularly persuasive. It begins with the observation that recent social theology has left the church looking backward and irrelevant – at most, a means to an end. He responds by going back to basics and restating the church's purpose: 'communicating to the rest of mankind the universally valid truths concerning God's liberating and redeeming work with fundamental openness . . . For this purpose, the Church only needs such visible structure as is necessary to permit her message and her genuineness to be proclaimed convincingly in the world.'[36] The church's basic 'structure' is the obedience of its servants, especially its ordained ministers. This obedience reflects 'something of that absolute unity which characterises the society of the divine Persons, in which nothing is private, where there are no divisions and no rivalries, but where the principle of unity is a love which encompasses and overrides all individuality.'[37] Though God's grace is present outside the church, this is the *source* of that out-flowing grace. For this is 'the community of those for whom the Word has not grown cold and become just abstract doctrine, but is the living personal presence of the Trinity, articulated in their life of brotherly love and a communion which is both sacramental and existential. Whenever in the world such a community exists, there is the source whence the world's true liberation begins.'[38]

Another Roman Catholic thinker who aroused Williams' interest was Thomas Merton, a Trappist monk who had become a well-known writer. He was a very 1960s sort of monk, interested in peace issues and Buddhism and critical of his Church's authoritarian tendencies. Shortly before his death in 1968, he strongly criticised US policy in Vietnam. With his fusion of traditional spirituality and radical engagement in the world's problems, Merton was the sort of figure who might have pulled Williams towards Rome. He showed that the contemplative life could seem relevant, realistic, contemporary. He had lived in England as a young man and was critical of its established Church, calling it 'a class religion, the cult of a special society and group, not even of a whole nation, but of the ruling minority of a nation.'[39]

> The Church of England depends, for its existence, almost entirely on the solidity and conservatism of the English ruling class . . . The English cling to their Church the way they cling to their King and their old schools: because of a big, vague, sweet complex of subjective dispositions regarding the English countryside, old castles and cottages, games of cricket in the long summer afternoons, tea-parties on the Thames, croquet, roast-beef, pipe-smoking, the Christmas panto, *Punch* and the London *Times* and all those other things the mere thought of which produces a kind of warm and inexpressible ache in the English heart.[40]

Amen. When the undergraduate Williams read this, perhaps it stirred a bit of Celtic resentment: why was he supporting the Church of the arrogant English, when there was an ecclesiastical world elsewhere? And he had now realised that Roman Catholic theology was far more philosophically sophisticated than that of Anglicanism or any other denomination. As we shall shortly see, it was far quicker to adapt to the philosophical developments of the mid twentieth century, and in Britain the Benedictines and the Dominicans were the pioneers. For Williams the theology and spirituality of Roman Catholicism were inextricable.

Another important strain of Roman Catholic influence is as much aesthetic as theological in the strict sense: it is represented above all by the Welsh artist and poet, David Jones. He was influenced by Eric Gill, whom we encountered in the Prologue. He developed Gill's discovery that art is sacramental and that its most basic form is ritual. This primal religious art form has the power to re-present, to make something present and alive again. The truth of Roman Catholicism lay in its awareness of this, its ability to read the world in sacramental terms, and its commitment to the actual, created world:

In contrast with some beliefs the belief of the Catholic Church commits its adherents, in a most inescapable manner, to the body and the embodied; hence to history, to locality, to epoch and site . . . [This] precludes the ersatz, and tends to a certain mistrust of the unembodied concept.[41]

In such a church, 'the Incarnation and the Eucharist cannot be separated; the one thing being analogous to the other. If one binds us to the animalic the other binds us to artefacture and both bind us to *signa*, for both are a showing forth of the invisible under visible signs.'[42] But is this a version of sacramentalism more suited to artists than responsible churchmen? We shall later see that Williams is drawn to an *anarchic* account of sacramentalism whose compatibility with ecclesiastical order is, to put it mildly, questionable.

Liberation theology

1968, Williams' first year as a theology student, was the year in which the movement known as liberation theology was launched in South America. Before we examine it, something ought to be said about the wider theological trend.

The idea that Christianity's real purpose is the transformation of this world can be traced back to the fourteenth century, but its first significant expressions come with the Radical Reformation of the sixteenth century. Thomas Müntzer adapted Lutheranism to lead a chiliastic peasants' revolt. Chiliasm, or millenarianism, is the belief that the Kingdom of God must be brought about by political means. Such thought was of course violently denounced by the mainstream Reformers as well as the Roman Church. Yet Protestantism continued to inspire such thought, for example during England's Civil War.

In the eighteenth and nineteenth centuries such thought of course took primarily secular form, most obviously in Marx. But it was also central to Protestant theology (largely thanks to Hegel). In the twentieth century the central figure is Barth. On one level, he reacted against religious socialism as essentially liberal, but on another level he incorporated it into his theology of divine transformation, of God's revolutionary 'Yes' to humanity.

During the 1960s, a few theologians were re-stating the case for a this-worldly eschatology. The trend began in the early 1960s with the work of the German theologian Wolfhart Pannenberg, who emphasised Christianity's commitment to 'universal history', seen in eschatological terms. But it was his colleague Jürgen Moltmann who was most influential; his book of 1964, *Theology of Hope*, launched a vogue for 'political theology'.

It was in Latin America that this trend really took off. Since the Cuban revolution of 1959, Marxism was widespread throughout the region, and some Roman Catholic priests began to sympathise. A group of theologians interpreted Vatican II as a green light to develop their own 'contextual' theology, first formulated at the 1968 Conference of Latin American Bishops. The basic insight was that salvation must be understood in political terms – as salvation from poverty and oppression. Conventional academic theology was charged with being ahistorical, and evasive of hard political choices. Theology could not be neutral, it had to be committed to the poor.

Its classic expression was Gutiérrez's book of 1969, *A Theology of Liberation*, which boldly affirmed the validity of Marxism as a theological tool, and urged a 'Utopian' understanding of the Kingdom of God. Most of these theologians were reluctant to challenge the Church too directly, but it was obvious that liberation theology was a threat to orthodox ecclesiology.

In the mid 1970s, such thought was hugely influential upon academic theology, though the influence was very often indirect and unstated. But the movement itself was running out of steam, failing to develop into a powerful new theological force. In 1984 the Vatican condemned its excesses, which hastened its demise.

Williams was critically sympathetic: as we shall see, he felt that left-wing Anglo-Catholicism could learn from liberation theology. But he was wary of liberation theology's rhetorical excesses. In an article of 1977 he refers to 'the doctrinaire inanities of some contemporary catholic Marxist writers', and warns against forgetting the doctrine of original sin.[43] But in another article of the same year he shows sympathy with the wider trend: protest at injustice 'witnesses to a "possible future", the knowledge that things might be otherwise, a new world: in this sense, God is the future (as Jürgen Moltmann and others have put it), the possibility of reconciliation. And the protest of compassion is his effective presence in the world, and so, in itself, a step towards the realisation of that possibility.'[44]

In the early 1980s, liberation theology often informs Williams' rhetoric. In an article of 1984 he insists that 'liberation' cannot be confined to a purely spiritual sense: liberation theology rightly shows us that 'the new humanity comes into being in history, in specific conditions.'[45] The movement's use of Marxism does not discredit it: indeed the church must be open to 'non-theological analyses of its context, if it is to avoid compromising its own calling to catholicity.'[46]

In the same year he insists that the situation in South Africa requires an explicitly political theology: to try to evangelise the black population is misguided, if it distracts from the political struggle. Perhaps Latin American liberation theology supplies a valid model, he suggests. Perhaps the church should be committed to 'the business of raising critical awareness, training in co-operative and self-supportive skills and the exploration of appropriate "gestures" in defiance of the status quo (boycotts and so on)'.[47]

And the following year he undertakes such a 'gesture' himself, though for a different cause. On Ash Wednesday 1985, he was arrested with a few others for breaking into a Cambridgeshire airbase, RAF Alconbury, a site of nuclear missiles.

In the opinion of a friend from undergraduate days who became an advocate of liberation theology, Williams' sympathy was only ever lukewarm. 'I've always felt Rowan is deeply conservative at heart. He never really subscribed to liberation theology – to the idea that reflection on grassroots activity should be the starting-point of theology. In his own parochial experience he perhaps toyed with this idea but I think he fell back on old fashioned Christian socialism, its theology of incarnation. In the end he always affirmed the official tradition of the Church.'

Though he is wary of quasi-Marxist rhetoric, Williams learns from liberation theology to see the Gospel as an agent of historical change, and to suspect otherworldly evasions – but, as we shall now see, Marx is not the only philosopher who helps him to root his theology in historical reality.

A philosophical revolution

While Williams was an undergraduate, Cambridge was still trying to digest the work of one of its philosophy dons, who had died in 1951: Ludwig Wittgenstein. He is perhaps the single most important intellectual influence on Williams, despite not being a theologian.

Soon after the First World War, Wittgenstein was hailed as the enigmatic genius of logical philosophy. His thought helped to inspire Logical Positivism, a rigorously anti-metaphysical school of thought that declared all philosophy meaningless when it departed from analytical reasoning. The movement was hugely influential in Britain, especially with the publication of A. J. Ayer's *Language, Truth and Logic* in 1936. But by this time Wittgenstein, now teaching in Cambridge, had begun to rethink the relationship between language and truth.

He had discovered that language is rooted in particular practices. Words are meaningful because of how we use them. Language is at root social and practical rather than quasi-metaphysical. This directly relates to the key error of modern philosophy: it has tried to inhabit an abstract, disembodied realm. It has pretended that we are primarily rational agents. But matter precedes mind; we create meaning through our social lives. Wittgenstein brought to philosophy the gaze of an anthropologist: 'I want to regard man as an animal, as a primitive being to which one grants instinct but not ratiocination – as a creature in a primitive state.'

He was fascinated by theology, and considered its familiar problems in a strange new way: how does religious language *work*, what is it *doing*? He was himself an eccentric, *angst*-ridden Christian, who could not accept any form of organised religion. The unsightly term 'devout sceptic' is for once apt: he was a sort of angry hermit, pondering religious and philosophical questions with gloomy, and rather violent, intensity. He felt called to purge philosophy of 'muddle', to save us from talking pretentious rubbish.

He took great exception to conventional philosophical theology. It talked as if God could theoretically be proved, as if the question of religious truth was something that could be settled by cleverness. But a religion is not a set of quasi-philosophical truth-claims; it is a way of living, an all-encompassing form of human existence. For example, to say 'God is love' or 'Jesus is alive' cannot be subjected to rational scrutiny any more than the gestures that may accompany such words, such as kneeling or looking upwards. Wittgenstein said, 'Christianity is not a doctrine but a description of something that actually happens.'

He was in effect warning theologians not to imitate the methods of philosophy. Instead, they should understand Christianity as a particular set of practices, or as a distinctive 'language-game'. In a sense, the theologian should be like an anthropologist, describing the particular patterns of the community's life, its rituals, and reflecting on the internal logic of faith.

This emphasis on the practical reality of religion entails an emphasis on its social character. If we see religion in practical terms, as a piece of human culture, then we cannot escape the anthropologist's insight that human meaning is at root social. In all forms of human culture, society precedes the individual. The proof of this is language: each of us uses a language that already exists, that is taught to us by our group. A private language is inconceivable. As we shall see, this critique of religious individualism influenced Williams hugely. He associated it with Marx's insight that meaning derives from humanity's creative work, which is always a social phenomenon, and also with Eastern Orthodoxy's priority of the social. Modernity has exalted the isolated individual who stands apart from social processes in order to think pure thoughts: from the Christian perspective no less than the Marxist perspective, he is a lost soul.

Most of the first theologians to take Wittgenstein seriously were Roman Catholics, some of whom had been his pupils. One of these was Cornelius Ernst, who belonged to Oxford's Dominican community. By the late 1960s this community had become a major force in British theology, from which Williams learned a huge amount during the next decade – especially from Herbert McCabe and Fergus Kerr. Another important Roman Catholic mediator of Wittgenstein (and Marx and others) was Nicholas Lash, Williams' Cambridge colleague in the 1980s. One former colleague sees the influence of Lash as decisive: 'Whenever I read Rowan, it's Nicholas's voice I hear.'

Williams also got his Wittgenstein by another means. It happened that the leading school of Wittgensteinian philosophers was Welsh – founded by Wittgenstein's pupil Rush Rhees. This Welsh connection seems to be surprisingly important. According to one of Williams' former pupils, 'Rowan kind of thinks of Wittgenstein as a Welsh bard.' This remark makes a bit more sense in the light of the thought of David Jones, and also the poetry of R. S. Thomas. The depiction of faith in Thomas' poetry is thoroughly Wittgensteinian; it focuses on the outward forms of prayer, and implies that this is all that we have, and that it is enough. Christianity entails a sort of brutal psychological and philosophical realism; it asks us to be satisfied with the *language* of God, the outward acts in which he is signified. Williams seems to detect this pathos in Wittgenstein; to see him as a sort of latter-day Desert Father perhaps, leading us away from the illusions surrounding faith.

As we shall see later on, Wittgenstein was an important influence on the major form of postmodern theology that emerged during the 1980s. His emphasis on 'grammar' was used to present Christianity as a distinctive 'language' that can be neither proved nor disproved. This position has been called 'Wittgensteinian fideism'. Its main application, as we shall see, was in a reassertion of the primacy of ecclesiology; an insistence that the practices of the Christian community are the foundation of theology.

It is worth noting that Wittgenstein himself might have had a few qualms about this application of his work. Though deeply sympathetic to Christian faith, he could not support any church. He found conventional religion essentially presumptuous, an affront to intellectual honesty. He dissuaded his friend Drury from becoming an Anglican priest: in the end he could not quite condone the traditional practices: 'For all you and I can tell, the religion of the future will be without any priests or ministers. I think one of the things that you and I have to learn is that we have to live without the consolation of belonging to a Church.'[48] He certainly did not mean to establish a new basis for theology in the ritual life of a worshipping community, to help churches justify their practices. On one level it is ironic that this enigmatic philosopher should be used by those wanting to promote a conservative emphasis on ecclesiology as the basis of theology. On the other hand, it is worth asking whether theologians who are seriously influenced by Wittgenstein are really such conservative ecclesiologists as they claim – and as we shall see, Williams is the prime example.

Wittgenstein's philosophy tied in with a wider trend that questioned the rational assumptions of modern thought, whose godfather is Nietzsche. 'Postmodernism' follows Nietzsche's rejection of the idea of rational, objective truth; his insistence that there are only various attempts at using language to exercise power. This sounds fundamentally atheistic, anti-theological. But many have seen this intellectual climate as an opportunity for theology. 'Postmodern theology', which is now the academic orthodoxy, is based in this idea. 'Modernity' was bad for theology; it tied it to the Enlightenment ideal of humanistic rationality and led it to disdain actual religious practice as irrational, primitive. The demise of modernism can therefore point Christians back to the social and traditional foundations of their faith.

Williams was of course influenced by postmodernism in general, but the central figure is certainly Wittgenstein. To him is attributed the watershed insight of modern religious thought: the 'essence of Christianity' lies *on the surface*, in the actual practices that define Christian communities – breaking bread together and so on. These practices are not inferior to the theories and doctrines that Christians espouse – they are actually superior. The attempt to locate the 'real' meaning of Christianity somewhere other than these basic practices is an error – a heresy.

CHAPTER TWO

OXBRIDGE

IN 1971 WILLIAMS was awarded a starred first in theology. He proceeded to Oxford, where he began research into Russian Orthodox theology. When he arrived he already spoke fluent Russian; his supervisor, Donald Allchin, is reputed to have declared that there was nothing he could teach his new student.

Someone who met him at this time recalls that he was 'appallingly intelligent, utterly confident and self-possessed, and yet at the same time [he] managed to be unassuming, unpretentious and likeable. It made you sick.' Others recall that he was coolly ambitious, right from the start of his theological career: careful not to waste his opportunities and contacts, careful not to say or do anything that could later count against him.

On the subject of youthful ambition: in 1973 an undergraduate law student and amateur rock musician was developing a strong interest in Christian socialism – the genesis of his political vocation. Perhaps at some Oxford discussion group – maybe on the need for disestablishment, or the iniquity of US foreign policy – Williams met the man who would one day appoint him to Canterbury. (If so, one imagines Williams flinching at the public-schoolboy enthusiasm with which Blair might have simplified the social gospel.)

Williams' commitment to the Church of England was still not complete at this point. Almost right until his ordination in 1977 he was looking very seriously at both Orthodoxy and Roman Catholicism, and gaining extensive experience of these traditions. In particular he became a regular visitor of Quarr Abbey on the Isle of Wight, and found a confessor in the prior, Joseph Warrilow – a Zosima figure, perhaps. He was positioning himself as a quintessential Catholic, on the intersection of Anglo-Catholicism, Roman Catholicism and Orthodoxy.

But of course Anglicanism afforded the largest opportunity for engagement, and advancement. In these years Williams became involved with politically radical Anglo-Catholicism. In 1974 a group was formed that sought to revive Anglo-Catholicism's social conscience. The Jubilee Group was founded by Ken Leech, a vicar in the East End of London, as a support group for other priests of similar views. One of the founders was an Oxford chaplain who knew Williams; he invited him to write a manifesto for the group. Williams' offering shows how he was importing the insights of Russian Orthodoxy into the Anglo-Catholic scene. It opened with a quotation from Nikolay Fyodorov: 'Our social programme is the dogma of the Holy Trinity.'

> We are committed to the struggle for justice, liberty and peace, not because of some secondary interest in social theory, but because of the very foundation of the Catholic Faith. We believe that man is made in the image of the Triune God, and is therefore social; that in Christ he is restored to his full capacity for social being. We believe that man is called to share the life of the Holy Trinity, the life of love and communion. We cannot, therefore, feign neutrality, or remain uncritical, in the face of a society based upon the ruthless pursuit of private gain and unlimited consumption. The institutionalised egotism of all forms of capitalism, including the Soviet collectivised form, must be challenged by Catholic Christians, if we are to remain faithful to the whole Gospel of Christ . . .

'We must make our stand', he concludes, 'with the oppressed, with the movement for liberation throughout the world.' The rhetoric is careless by his later standards – but he was only twenty-four. What stands out is the will to root a theology of liberation in traditional doctrinal theology, and particularly ecclesiology. If the church understands itself rightly, it *already* has this agenda. His manifesto was judged too triumphalistic, but he remained linked to the group for well over a decade, writing and co-editing pamphlets for them.

In his mid-to-late-twenties his conception of faith was affected by spells of depression. This deepened his attachment to mystical theology, particularly the 'negative' or 'apophatic' tradition that emphasises God's unknowability, and the inadequacy of all religious formulae. It also led, ultimately, to a deeper sense of the totality of God's redemption of his creation. He later recalled that in these years he gained 'a sense that darkness, confusion and sin in my own life had been confronted and dealt with by Christ on the cross – I learned that there was no corner of that darkness not explored by Christ.'[1] He also acquired a new understanding of the way in which the Christian participates in the very being of God in the act of worship: 'I can remember really quite vividly in my late twenties realising almost for the first time why the gift of the Spirit in saying "*Abba*, Father" was really the hinge of all theology – that was what made sense of talking of God as Trinity, and sense of our being made in the image and likeness of God.'[2] This tied in with an emphasis in early Eastern theology that we have already remarked on: the idea that, through the gift of faith, God effects the *deification* of humanity. The Fall is overcome, humanity is made new. But what, in practice, did Williams understand by this? It sounds like a sort of utopianism, focused on the church – a dangerously high ecclesiology. Perhaps he began to see his attachment to the Church of England, with all its obvious difficulties and failings, as a useful counterweight to this line of thought, a check on his attraction to this ecclesiological idealism.

In 1975, soon after his doctoral thesis was passed, he secured a teaching job at the Community of the Resurrection, the semi-monastic Anglo-Catholic training college in Mirfield, Yorkshire. He was the only layman among the teaching staff, yet was fully involved in the community's liturgical life, and preached as well as lectured. A Mirfield colleague recalls that his interest in Orthodoxy lent him a rather exotic aura, confirmed by the beard and deep voice (it is strange to remember that he was only 26!). But in fact he was very seriously considering becoming a Roman Catholic scholar-monk, either at Downside, which he had often visited, or on the Continent, where there were more academic monasteries. He came close to testing a vocation, but decided that he could not accept papal infallibility, even provisionally.

He certainly had a priestly calling: he just wasn't sure which Church it was to. A sermon he delivered at Mirfield in 1976 reveals something of the passionate idealism involved in this calling: 'Christian life, Christian ministry, is not a matter of calculation and of realism ... [Christ] calls us to abandon policy and protectiveness, to attend to and respond to his Word sounding in all human hurt, to be wounded and find out our helplessness . . . He will not wipe the tears from our eyes until we have learned to weep.'[3] Even before his ordination he was a powerful preacher, a performance poet of reflective Christian passion. And even before he went to Mirfield he had, as a colleague recalls, 'a network of pastoral relationships who often came to visit him at weekends.' Actually getting ordained was rather a formality in some respects.

It happened in 1977, when he started teaching at the Cambridge ordination college, Westcott House. Ordinands are meant to spend two years in residential training – this was waived for Williams; his time at Mirfield was deemed sufficient. Without overstating the point, it is necessary to note that ordination into Anglicanism has the appearance of a fall-back option, hurriedly embraced. About a year before he was ordained, perhaps less, he was thinking that his spiritual destiny probably lay elsewhere. To put it crudely, he took Anglican orders on the rebound from his flirtation with Rome. But he seems not to have regretted the decision. Some years later one of his doctoral students was wavering between Roman Catholicism and Anglicanism: he advised him that the sheer difficulty of Anglicanism was salutary for a theologian; becoming a Roman Catholic would be too easy.

What was his opinion of the Church he had pledged to serve? He felt that it had entered a particularly challenging period. It had recently gained greater autonomy: General Synod, founded in 1970, had assumed control over worship and doctrine in 1974. This was a good thing in Williams' eyes, but it was accompanied by a dangerous impulse towards modernisation for its own sake. In particular he was uneasy at the process of liturgical modernisation. He retained a strong attachment to the old Prayer Book: he would continue to enjoy celebrating the old service for years to come. He later lamented the 'wrong direction' taken by liturgical modernisers in the 1970s – towards less memorable liturgies, and a tendency to functionalism, a forgetfulness of 'the way in which these things bed themselves in people's minds.'[4]

He was also uneasy at the growing appetite for doctrinal innovation. The theology of the 1960s had led to a widespread suspicion of traditional doctrine. This mood was represented in the 1976 report of the Doctrine Commission of the Church of England, *Christian Believing*. He later wrote that this report 'probably represented the high-water mark of [Anglicanism's] detachment from

doctrinal tradition'.[5] A new level of doctrinal liberalism was emerging in academic theology, most obviously with *The Myth of God
Incarnate*, a collection of ultra-liberal essays, in 1977.

The Church was also struggling to understand its changing
relationship to the national culture – Williams' Welshness afforded
him some distance here, a detachment from the awkward identity-
blend that affects every English Anglican. When the nation
celebrated the Queen's Silver Jubilee in the year of his ordination,
he could look on with a Nonconformist's detachment – his
own Anglicanism was not implicated in this rather questionable
carry-on.

Or was it? He did not explicitly address the issue, but the
Church of England's establishment seems to have troubled him.
This emerges in an essay of 1984. The Church's failure to oppose
nuclear weapons was 'a happy reassurance to the government that
the established church could still be relied upon'.[6] And parliament's
attempt to block liturgical reform showed that 'the constitutional
question of the rights of the General Synod of the Church of
England . . . is by no means settled in the minds of many.'[7] (At this
time conservative Anglicans such as Enoch Powell were challenging the Church's right to legislate independently of parliament.)
So is the Church of England, despite its recent reforms, still defined
by erastianism? Williams admits that the Church is historically
complicit with 'a theory of absolute sovereign right vested in the
monarch and the state apparatus'.[8] Even nineteenth-century
Christian socialism was absolutely implicated in this model: 'its
leaders were basically conservative monarchists, with a markedly
hierarchical view of society.'[9] But in practice the nineteenth
century saw the end of 'the religiously monolithic state' –
Anglicanism is now, in effect, based in a federalist political model.
'We might add that the development of the Anglican Communion
itself in the last 150 years shows just this implicit move towards
pluralism and detachment from the monolithic state.'[10]

What this line of argument amounts to is a claim that establishment has lost its negative aspect, that the Church's original
political determination is no longer relevant, even though it for-
mally abides. The negative side of establishment is *no longer real*. But
Williams is trying to persuade himself of what he has trouble really
believing. A few years later, as we shall see, he worries about an
established church's 'endorsement of the *de facto* structures and

constraints of the life of a sovereign state'.[11] But in general he seems to have felt that the Church of England was moving away from establishment, slowly but surely – and that this awkward process was not quite his concern as an outsider. Were he English (or were the Welsh Church still established), he might have had to face the issue more squarely.

He served as chaplain as well as tutor at Westcott House, thus gaining his first official pastoral experience counselling students. In 1980 he became a university lecturer. Yet he was reluctant to let his priestly identity be replaced by an academic one; he refused election to a college fellowship that carried no pastoral duties. One of his colleagues at the divinity faculty identified him as 'one of those theologians whose life is centred on their prayer'. Indeed, he used to begin his lectures with a prayer, until there were complaints and he was asked to stop the practice. And it was partly to remind himself of his primary calling that he now volunteered to serve in a parish just outside Cambridge, living in the curate's house for three years with his new wife (he married in 1979). He contemplated leaving Cambridge altogether, to be a parish priest in Wales. But the academic world held on to him for another decade: in 1984 he became Fellow and Dean of Clare College, and in 1986 he returned to Oxford, to become Lady Margaret Professor of Divinity.

It is obvious from this biographical sketch that his commitment to the church is beyond doubt. It is his life, his setting. Yet his difficulty in deciding on a denomination is surely significant; it suggests that his true allegiance is to the church in general rather than any particular institution, and that he sees the need to join a particular church as a regrettable necessity. He yearns for a non-denominational, supra-institutional Catholicism.

In what follows I am not questioning his commitment to the church (or to its Anglican form). I am suggesting that, within his unambiguously committed role, Williams develops a surprisingly critical approach to ecclesiology. It is as if he cannot silence a nagging voice that calls into question the very basis of ecclesiology. I am reading his theology as the attempted appeasement of this voice.

Critical spirituality

In 1979 Williams' first book, *The Wound of Knowledge*, was published. It originates in the course he had been teaching, first at Mirfield

and then at Westcott House, on the history of Christian spirituality. Though the book is not primarily concerned with the
church, it offers some useful clues.

It begins with the observation that the Christian account of
spirituality is marked by a certain realism, and even materialism, for
'it becomes increasingly difficult in the Christian world to see the
ultimately important human experience as an escape into the transcendent, a flight out of history and the flesh.'[12] The experience of
God, he says,

> [is] mediated in the objective form of a shared life and lan-
> guage, a public and historical community of men and women,
> gathering to read certain texts and perform certain acts. That
> which transmits God's question from age to age is the Church
> (perhaps the Church can only be defined in some such way, as
> the bearer of that question; and conversely, it might be said that
> whatever bears that question is the Church); in this vastly
> diverse community, extending so widely in time and space, are
> the first resources for each person to live with the question.[13]

He thus defines church in anthropological rather than strictly theological terms. He does not offer a high ecclesiology – of the
church as the body of Christ – but presents the church from a
human perspective, as a diverse collection of distinctive cultural
forms. The definition of church as 'whatever bears [God's] question'
suggests that conventional ecclesiology might be far too narrow.
This impression is supported by his preliminary sketch of Christian
origins. The Gospel puts all religious and political systems in doubt;
to believe in this God 'is to believe in an anarchic mercy that
ignores order, rank and merit.'[14]

The book's core argument is that Christian faith is not a
secure possession but an awareness of a lack. He shows how Luther
agrees with Catholic mystics in this respect: the Christian's inner
experience necessarily points beyond itself, for it is defined by its
apprehension of the absence of God. It follows that no intellectual,
mystical or ritual formula can capture God.

In his conclusion he quotes the Dominican theologian
Cornelius Ernst. The core Christian experience, says Ernst, is both
positive and negative: 'If the experience were not *both at once*, it
would split apart into an insipid humanism of progress (or a revolutionary arrogance), or an esoteric mystique of world-abnegation.'

Williams calls this 'the heart of classical Christian spirituality'. We are called 'to the creation of new humanity in the public, the social and historical, world – to the transformation of behaviour and relationship, knowing God in acting and making' – but in the knowledge that this enterprise is provisional, and in a sense impossible, for the cross puts every religious achievement in question; it shows that 'there is no place for the Word in the world.'[15]

The experience of God's absence is therefore a *critical* resource, a means of suspecting the cultural claims of this religion, of re-rooting it in the logic of the cross. Monasticism has performed this function: it has witnessed to 'the tension between this age and the age to come, to the *absence* of the Kingdom of God on earth. Karl Barth, no uncritical devotee of monasticism, allows that [it] may be seen as "a highly responsible and effective opposition to the world, and not least to a worldly Church".'[16] Any form of Christian culture that forgets the negativity enshrined in the cross, its judgement on all human religion, is inauthentic.

In his first book Williams displays an intense wariness towards any form of Christian triumphalism (the counter-cultural idealism of liberation theology is seen as a variant of this danger: he approvingly quotes Ernst's warning against 'revolutionary arrogance'). Christianity is constantly tempted to become a successful piece of human culture. This is inevitable, for it claims to offer something absolutely new – the transformation of human life. But it must remember the 'otherness' of this claim; its difference from any other such claim, its reference to an eschatological reality. The surest proof of this is to be found on the individual level: the tradition of apophatic Christian spirituality reminds us that this is not (or not straightforwardly) a religion of fulfilment, success, achievement, cultural progress. It is significant that Williams makes Luther central to his case, and also cites Barth: there is a Protestant dimension to his suspicion of religion (the influence of his teacher Donald MacKinnon is surely present here). Alongside the aesthetically-minded Catholicism is a starker religious vision: a colleague at this time recalls that he had 'a sombre side, a streak of residual Calvinism'.[17]

Re-thinking 'catholicity'

In 1981 Williams contributed to a volume of essays reflecting on the Anglican-Roman Catholic International Commission (ARCIC).

Hopes of moving towards reunion were strong in these years – the Pope had visited Britain in 1981 and had been warmly received by Archbishop Runcie.

Williams' essay, 'Authority and the Bishop in the Church', calls on the church to reflect on how it understands authority. Christians are obliged to face this thorny question, for catholicity means 'the mutual critical openness of the local body and the wider structure, the reciprocal nourishment offered by particular local communities. And if catholicity matters, structures of authority matter.'[18] But in this case authority must be determined by its distinctive context, by the church's goal – 'a particular vision of human welfare, harmony and fulfilment'.[19]

He now goes right back to basics and tries to describe the essence of the church, in relation to its origins. It is a community that is defined and guided by

> the 'paschal mystery' of the death and exaltation of Jesus: God's blameless servant is the victim of a paradigmatic act of violence and rejection, but God 'returns' him to the world as the ultimate and decisive symbol of undefeated compassion and inexhaustible creative resource. Upon this gift hangs the possibility of the existence of a shared life of gift: that is what the Church is created and constituted to be.
>
> So the 'goals' of the Church can be described in terms of the formation of a human community in which oppressive and diminishing relationships are transformed through the mediation of a controlling story or image. The human options available to the Church are limited by the force of this central symbol: cross and resurrection constitute an *authoritative* reality in the believing community. The Church's limits are defined at the most primary level by its reference to an event in which violent power is judged and grace and mutuality are declared to be the fundamental ways in which God lives and is shown in the world.[20]

He goes on to explain that Christian identity is defined not by 'any act of submission to an administrative structure, but . . . incorporation into a worshipping – a ritual–celebrating – group . . . If this is true, the simplest and most central "authority" in the Church is this authority of the *symbol*.'[21] But in practice, he goes on, this 'authority of the symbol' is mediated by the bishop:

If authority belongs primarily to the symbol, it belongs deriv-
atively to whoever gives that symbol concrete and coherent
form. In early Christian practice, *only* the bishop baptized, just
as only the bishop ordained, because it is only by reference to
the single figure in a district set apart to be *himself* a 'symbol'
accessible to all, related to all, not representing only a sector of
the community, that the actual limits of the Church can be
discerned. Pragmatically, the Church was those who assembled
round the bishop, those recognised by the bishop as having
placed their lives under the authority of the crucified and
risen Jesus.[22]

For Williams, then, the 'authority of the symbol' gives rise to the
authority of the bishop – it authorises him. For the bishop trans-
lates 'the authority of the symbol' into a concrete form of social
existence that is capable of uniting disparate groups of people. His
authority 'is an authority to unify'.[23] He enables the church's
'catholicity', meaning the dynamic of reciprocal influence between
the local unit and the whole. 'If a bishop is truly to unveil the
catholicity of the local church, he cannot depend for his ordination
only on the local and contemporary, he must visibly belong in a
community extended in time and space beyond the local.'[24]

The bishop (and, by extension, priest) is an intermediary
between the locality that he serves and the wider church. But in
practice unity between bishops is fragile – and this is how the papacy becomes theoretically justifiable: 'if the bishop's role as symbol of
unity defines his authority as authority to unify, the same is true of
the Pope: in the Church at large, the Pope's task is to refer all
Christians to the single catholic truth, the paschal symbol.'[25] There
is a certain logic to this solution, says Williams, but on the other
hand it moves us away from the local community, and so must be
subjected to a 'rigorous critique'.[26]

In his conclusion he reasserts that ecclesiastical authority is
rooted in 'a controlling symbol, liturgically appropriated'.[27] Does
this mean that the 'controlling symbol' is only accessible through
the church? Not quite: 'Receptivity to the symbol can involve us in
hearing its judgement from those who are marginal to the Church's
symbolic life – who are, rather, *marginalised* by the Church's failure
to be what it sacramentally says it is, the community of gift.'[28]
Famous examples of the marginalised include Kierkegaard, Peguy,

Simone Weil. But, he hastily insists, the sacramental life of the community is normative: 'we can only see such figures as authoritative if we already know and feel the contours of the paschal symbol from elsewhere – from the "ordinary" life of the baptizing and eucharistizing community.'[29] To exalt any of these outsiders as authoritative is 'merely romantic: the "authority" of heroic integrity alone provides no substantial basis for a Christian view of authority. The great isolated figures of Christian history are answerable to the same symbol we are all answerable to, and their stature is assessed by reference to that. Otherwise we have a multitude of "Vatican I" popes, not answerable to the Church at large . . .'[30]

In this essay Williams demonstrates the Protestantism within his Catholicism. This idea of the 'authoritative symbol' is not totally unlike the Protestant idea of the Word of God, a principle that precedes, and authorises, the church. But this 'symbol' is in practice inseparable from the church. So Williams *almost* promises that we can directly access Christianity's foundational symbol, and use it to re-think ecclesiology. But on closer inspection, it seems that one cannot fundamentally question the authority of the church, without setting oneself up as an autopope.

Before leaving this essay, it is worth noting how far removed his ecclesiastical idealism is from Anglican reality. The idea that the bishop's authority derives from the local congregation would seem to go against the reality of English history: Anglican episcopacy is surely rooted in a 'top-down' model of authority – it is inextricable from the power of the Crown. But Williams is not constrained by this history; his ideal of catholicity is closer to the early church, in which authority retained its local dimension, and Russian Orthodoxy, which seems to preserve this ideal.

It is also worth noting his mindfulness of the marginalised voices who call the church into question. The reference to Simone Weil is especially significant: he has frequently expressed admiration for the thought of this eccentric French Jewish socialist philosopher who converted to Christianity but spurned the church and finally, during the Second World War, starved herself to death. He is particularly attracted to her form of negative theology, her fear that every use of the word 'God' reeks of human ego, and that every religious institution is guilty of collective egotism. This intense sensitivity to the danger of idolatry is primarily what impresses Williams. 'To imagine God is, Weil implies, to conceive a state of affairs, a determination of circumstances, which will inevitably be conditioned by my needs, and will be a falsehood.'[31] Her quest for a pure religious sensibility entails a quasi-Buddhist acceptance of the world and a possibly masochistic respect for suffering, as that which reveals the true state of affairs. There is a highly ambiguous socio-political dimension: instead of wishing for an ideal society, we should accept the weakness of human beings, their need for 'roots'. We should learn to love them as they are rather than as we think they should be.

Resurrection

In Lent of 1982 he was invited by the Bishop of Stepney to give a series of addresses to clergy working in the East End of London. These formed the basis for his second book, *Resurrection*. The book attempts to expound the resurrection as 'the generative event at the source of the Church's life'.[32] The task of theology, he insists, is to refer the church back to this basis. Theology ought to 'criticise and test the Church's practice by reference to its professed allegiance to Jesus crucified and risen.'[33] This clearly ties in with what we have previously seen: the 'central symbol' of cross and resurrection underlies the church.

Williams' basic thesis is that a totally new sort of community arises in response to the apprehension of Easter. Its purpose is the corporate manifestation of God. As he puts it at one point, 'The believing community manifests the risen Christ: it does not simply talk about him, or even "celebrate" him. It is the place where he is shown.'[34]

> We become 'carriers' of the truthfulness of Jesus. The believer who lives in the furnace of this truth is being a witness to the rest of humanity of the possibility of living with truth – burning, but not consumed . . . In the Spirit, we are not only the recipients but the transmitters of hope, and our new identity is bound up with that destiny to transmit hope, to 'preach the gospel'.[35]

In the above, Williams displays an uncharacteristically Protestant emphasis upon the witness of the individual Christian (the influence of Barth seems clear). But then the emphasis returns to the community: it is 'the community of faith' that 'is charged with sharing this vision and this possibility of life with all the world'.[36] Indeed, the community replaces the individual prophet:

> In the Spirit, judgement is *constantly* to be pronounced upon 'the prince of this world', the dominant destructiveness in unredeemed human relations. It is not pronounced in isolated prophetic utterance: that model of the activity of 'Spirit' belongs to an older and less nuanced tradition. Instead it is pronounced in the characteristic life of the believing community. Just as Jesus himself embodies but does not pronounce the world's judgement . . . so with the Church, which is thus liable to the same rejection.[37]

Williams is asking us to see the community in terms that are more normally applied to the individual prophet. The church is a prophet – or rather the final prophet – in corporate, institutional form. The above analogy between Jesus and the church is more than an analogy; it implies that the church is the continuation of the incarnation. This is a traditional Catholic idea (it was restated at the turn of the twentieth century by the Anglo-Catholic theologian Charles Gore). Williams gives it a new twist: the church continues Christ's prophetic role, which is supra-verbal; ontological rather than functional. And because it does this, we no longer need individual prophets – for, in the form of the church, Christ himself is made present.

The church's message is synonymous with its own form of life, it would seem. But now Williams seems to question his own theory. Christian witness can entail cultural dissent, including dissent from Christian culture – for example, the early Christian hermits refused 'to identify "being a Christian" with belonging to a Christian family or a Christian society. The believing life can be lived without kin and without citizenship; if they disappear, belief need not.'[38] This somewhat undermines his main thesis, that the church is now God's definitive prophet. He hastens to say: 'Such a witness is, of course, a caveat for the rest of the Church rather than a judgement.' But that reassurance feels a bit hollow.

He now explains that the church must be intrinsically penitent – conscious of its own fallibility. And this is why the Eucharist is so central:

> [W]hen the Church performs the Eucharistic action, it is what it is called to be: the Easter community, guilty and restored, the gathering of those whose identity is defined by their new

relation to Jesus crucified and raised, who identify themselves as forgiven . . . It is an action which announces what the community's life means, where the roots of its understanding and its possibilities are; and as such it is a transforming, a re-creative act — a human activity radically open to the creative activity of God in Jesus Christ . . . It allows the source-event, the mystery of cross and resurrection, to become present again, and so opens itself to the rich resource of that event.[39]

The Eucharist is the climax, the consummation of the church; the moment at which it is 'open' to God. To put it differently, the Eucharist is seen as the symbolic core of the church, its signature tune, its 'brand-essence' (to borrow a bit of marketing-speak that Williams would flinch from). On one level, Williams' perspective is that of an anthropologist, explaining the social function of this rite.

His discussion now touches on the concept of catholicity. It does not mean an aspiration to uniformity, but to the church's mission to reach into every corner of human life — and this mission necessitates sensitivity to cultural diversity. The church will be 'tirelessly seeking new horizons in its own experience and understanding by engaging with this diversity, searching to see how the gospel is to be lived and confessed in new and unfamiliar situations; and doing this because of its conviction that each fresh situation is already within the ambience of Jesus' cross and resurrection, open to his agency, under his kingship.'[40]

But catholicity also means 'openness to the range and depth of the whole family of believers, past and present: tradition belongs with catholicity, and the rejection of the Christian past creates as many problems as any other kind of rejection.'[41] So catholicity means adaptability to every new situation, communion with all other Christians, and fidelity to the past. It sounds like an impossible ideal, cubed. The obvious question is whether the different forms of catholicity are compatible with each other — church history strongly suggests not.

Instead of acknowledging the impossibility of catholicity as he describes it, Williams speaks as if the church (but what church?) is capable of realising this ideal. He explains that ordained ministry is an agent of catholicity, as it links each congregation to the tradition and to the rest of the church, and also due to its capacity to rethink the church's boundaries and structures. On one level, this extreme idealism is intended as a reforming stance: to be truly catholic, the reader is meant to conclude, the church must change. But in practice he is also idealising the church in its empirical form. He demands so much of the church that in the end it is questionable whether he demands any fundamental re-direction at all.

He soon returns to an account of church that is wider than any institution:

> in the Church, by the Spirit, Jesus is found to be 'Lord', and the titles of supreme honour are given him. The Spirit enables Jesus to be named for what he is – in the life of the first small communities, in the liturgy, in the long and bitter doctrinal struggles of the early Church, in the protest of the monastic order, in the radical 'refusals' of Luther and the Reformation, in the costly askesis of the contemplative, and the simple gift of the martyr. In all these, Jesus is confessed, in word, symbol and act, as of unsurpassable meaning and inexhaustible resource: as Lord.[42]

In *what* church? This account transcends any particular institution. For the Spirit is always enabling *new* forms of the proclamation of the Lordship of Jesus – no institution can keep up with the Spirit. Church in this full sense is not an institution but an anarchic movement. Yet Williams wants to insist that this vision is compatible with the 'conservative' face of catholicity: the affirmation of church as the body of Christ. Williams is therefore promoting a disruptive and a conservative account of catholicity *at the same time*.

Realising the impossible?

In 1983 Williams wrote a short book called *The Truce of God*, which is partly concerned with advocating nuclear disarmament. His argument is based in an understanding of catholicity. The church cannot condone the world's Cold War division without 'undermining its own deepest reality. For the Church is itself a symbol – of the "catholic" love of God for his creation, the adaptability of his love to each and every creature . . .'[43] Soon he insists again that the church is catholic, meaning 'for all, adapting itself endlessly to human culture and to human need . . . When it is not catholic, it is not truly itself . . . And when it is, however sporadically and unsurely, catholic, it is a sacrament of peace . . .'[44] He admits the impossibility of the ideal: the church is 'never going to be completely itself while history lasts . . . However, the Church does exist – not perfectly, but still quite concretely. Within its own life it is found to be a sacrament, an effective, compelling symbol, of a humanity able to live by sharing and by loving, reverent mutual attention.'[45]

As in *Resurrection*, there is insufficient explanation of how catholicity relates to actual ecclesiastical institutions, and to the political situation of each church. To call the church a sacrament is to presuppose that it is a reasonably coherent entity, something that is visibly there. For surely an idea or aspiration cannot meaningfully be called a sacrament. The idea of the church as a sacrament, which had been enshrined in Vatican II, draws attention to the elusiveness of 'church'.

He considers Jesus' original vision of peace. It asked a question of Palestinian society:

> Can this society be a *catholic* society? The answer is that it cannot contain such a vision. Jesus is, as Bonhoeffer put it, 'edged out' to the cross; Jesus's followers are likewise squeezed out of their religious milieu into a new community without the familiar barriers. The Church is what is expelled by societies as they struggle with the challenge of God's peace.

Is this true of the established Church of England? One would like to hear more about the relationship between catholicity and real churches.

Towards the end of the book, he partially confronts the idealism of his account of catholicity: 'But of course it is not really enough to talk as though such a community already existed in any and every church group in the world. If we put the problem in these terms, it is plain that we have a great deal of work to do in making the Church more Church-like.'[46] He goes on to make a few modest proposals, principally that local churches should forge international links. But there is surely a category confusion here. To call for the church to be more church-like is to call for the impossible. 'We have a great deal of work to do in realising the impossible': an absurd understatement – and overstatement.

The core problem is the huge semantic muddle surrounding 'the church'. Not only does it refer to an ideal as well as a reality: it refers to various ideals and various realities. The common explanation is that there is a visible church and an invisible church. The

visible church is the flawed and divided reality on earth; the invisible church is the idealised essence of church which will never be
clearly revealed in this world.

But this is grammatically messy. The first half of the equation,
'the visible church', is deeply muddled. Does it refer to every single
institution claiming to be Christian? If so, is it meaningful to
bundle them all together into a collective term? Or does it mean
the main churches which claim ancient lineage? For a Roman
Catholic, 'the visible church' primarily refers to his own Church.
For an Anglo-Catholic, the term seems to refer to a vague con-
glomerate of his own Church and the Roman Church, with the
others tacked on. The concept of 'the visible church' is basically
unhelpful. It speaks about an abstraction as if it is an unambiguous
tangible reality.

And of course the other, idealised, sense of 'church' is no less
confusing: it contains many jostling ideals. On one level it means an
idealised and finally triumphant version of a particular institution –
especially in the case of Roman Catholicism. On another level it
means the authentic essence of each historical church. It might also
mean something less 'religious': the true movement for the world's
redemption, that is not confined to church history. As we have seen,
this last meaning is certainly present in Williams' thought; what he
means by 'church' often seems to blur with the Kingdom of God
itself.

This semantic mega-muddle is hard to uproot. For it is cus-
tomary to make a virtue of this vagueness: to lump together one's
own institution with the ideal, as if such confusion is a sign of faith.

From what we have seen so far, Williams wants to blur the
meanings of 'church'. For he wants to affirm two things at once: the
institutional reality, with its distinctive ritual and social practices,
and the vision at the heart of this cultural form: an anarchic, utopian vision of God's universal, unbounded Kingdom. The two are by
definition incompatible. For it is impossible for any institution,
however holy, to realise this vision. If a church is a coherent society
it must have boundaries, it must be limited. It will necessarily take
itself seriously, defend its traditions, police its boundaries – and
therefore compromise its vision of universal peace.

Williams wants to suggest that the church is the fusion of its
real and its ideal forms. The ideal of church is realised in the tangible reality. But surely this leads to the 'ideological' justification

of what exists, the claim that the church as we know it is ideal? What prevents this, says Williams, is the sacramental core, in which the ideal becomes really present. 'The eucharist is always a celebration of the new humanity, the "community of gift" between God and human beings and between human beings themselves.'[47] If the church can base itself in the Eucharist, then it is a benign rather than ideological fusion of reality and ideality.

An essay of 1983 is a clear statement of the eucharistic basis of Williams' Catholicism: 'the orthodox Christian community identifies itself not simply and absolutely by some mode of organisation, but by gathering to do certain things. Orthodoxy is inseparable from sacramental practice.'[48] What the community supremely does is to re-present Easter, but Williams puts this in a wider, sociological context:

> Orthodoxy (any orthodoxy) involves shared ritual enactments, crystallisations of the kind of life the ideology serves: the Christian sacraments, above all the Eucharist, show the believer engaged with and challenged by the source event of faith, engaging in 'cross and resurrection', and so making the paradigm his or her own, making the life lived from that sacrament a reflection, a kind of translation of the paradigm. And so . . . every believing life becomes, in some measure, part of 'orthodox tradition'.

The virtue of Catholic tradition is to present us with a broad range of such 'translations' – he names Polycarp, Augustine, Wesley, Edith Stein, Janani Luwum. The Catholic performance of the Eucharist is informed by 'the communion of saints', by the memory of their diverse appropriation of the paradigm. The church, or 'the eucharistic Church', is conscious of cultural diversity and therefore resists the urge to divinise any particular cultural form. He seems to envisage a sort of dialectical process – through experience of cultural diversity, of countless translations into countless contexts, the tradition apprehends its essence (which is of course never directly available). The church, he goes on, will attend to 'the witness and gift of other ages and cultures and the baffling diversities of Christian thought and styles of living':

> Which is why Catholics speak of ministry in the Church as also sacramental, the effective present symbol of continuities: once again, a theological interest in apostolicity of ministry

ought to be something which guarantees a concern for keeping questions open, a sensitivity to the variety of Christian
experience in history – and which thus regularly unsettles
uncritically hierarchical models of leadership in the Church,
since the symbol it serves involves a story of the inversion of
normal authority patterns . . . It is sad that – like 'orthodoxy'
itself – this whole issue has been distorted into questions about
power, purity and exclusion.[49]

A high theology of ministry is a necessary means to remaining in
touch with tradition, and therefore also remaining true to the sacramental core. The priest has a special role: mediating Catholic tradition to the local congregation, so that the particular congregation
is not trapped in its subjectivity:

> Catholic orthodoxy insists on the centrality of shared symbols,
> on the essential importance of multiform narratives to inter-
> pret the focal event, and on signs of living continuity in time
> and space – sacraments, saints, apostolic ministry, all of the
> means of freeing us from the prison of a 'given' social
> perspective.[50]

Of course there will be a dubious element in all this culture, but
Catholic tradition is the most reliable 'carrier' of the eucharistic
essence, by which this religious culture is endlessly judged. When
the Eucharist is faithfully performed, the negative aspect of the
institutional church drops away.

The core of Williams' ecclesiology, to put it rather naively, is
the fact that he really believes in the Eucharist. This rite actualises
the essence of Christianity, the remaking of humanity through
the cross and resurrection of Jesus. The fact that the Eucharist
'works' is the justification of church; it is the reason that we bother
with the endlessly difficult and perhaps contradictory business of
ecclesiology.

Faith, language, culture

Williams' ecclesiology must be understood in relation to his innovative approach to the philosophy of religion. This is exemplified in
an article of 1985 on the work of his Cambridge colleague Don
Cupitt, whose ultra-liberalism we have already considered.

Cupitt attacks the idea that religious language refers to something 'out there', something beyond itself. He calls for an explicitly 'non-realist' theology, that admits that humanity creates its own values, including religious ones. The problem with this, says Williams, is that 'God' becomes the function of a human end; the human will becomes the highest authority. Authentic religious discourse tells the opposite story:

> the grammar of faith has to do with yielding self-interest to God's glory, with praise, the ascription of worth to what we have no control over. A religious discourse which denied . . . the extra-subjective reality of God would hardly be intelligible. The element of praise would vanish, and the dimension of gratuity – or even what we might call play.[51]

As the phrase 'the grammar of faith' suggests, Williams draws heavily on Wittgenstein. Cupitt's 'non-realism' is seen as exalting the abstract autonomous individual, and denying 'our belonging in a context, our social and natural being':[52]

> Acknowledging our inescapable insertion into community and what some awkwardly call 'linguality' is not automatically to settle for bad faith. It is rather a condition for the necessary realism (in the looser sense of the word) which shows us ourselves as neither wholly finished nor wholly free, as having a body, a language *and* an imagination: a presence to nature and society, *and* a capacity for history and personality.[53]

This is the heart of Williams' postmodernism: the insistence that we are formed by communities, with their particular conceptual languages. Theology cannot jettison the idea of God's objective existence because of the obvious philosophical problems it brings. Instead it must seek to understand this claim in socio-linguistic terms, to understand how it relates to various distinctive cultural practices.

A few years later he argues for an affinity between Wittgenstein and Bonhoeffer (a cynic might wonder if this is an attempt to increase Wittgenstein's Christian credibility, by linking him with a kosher martyr). If theologians are to take Wittgenstein seriously, he begins,

> We shall need to rethink much of what we habitually say about 'authentic' or 'interior' prayer, about acts and intentions,

about mortality and eternal life; theology must rediscover itself as a language that assists us in being mortal, living in the constraints of a finite and material world without resentment.[54]

Wittgenstein and Bonhoeffer, he argues, both question the idea of an authentic inner self, which is one of modernism's key assumptions. They suggest that meaning resides in surfaces, in cultural practices, in ordinary symbol-laden language. Does this mean that 'inner experience' must be jettisoned as a piece of false consciousness? No, but it should be re-conceived: not as an end in itself but as a resource for the better use of religious language, which is an essentially public activity. The inner life as an end in itself is an un-Christian idea.

The essential point is that everything is cultural – even the 'inner life'. There is something vaguely Zen about this: we should renounce the desire for a pure realm of 'religious truth', a desire which philosophy inherits. We should be satisfied with the rather crude things that we demonstrably have: the language, the practices. Religious practice is not a flawed attempt to do something supra-cultural, such as commune with God or be saved or know the metaphysical truth. There is nothing outside of the performance, the cultural text, the doing and saying. It follows that the church should be seen as a cultural phenomenon: it does not exist *in* cultural history, it exists *as* cultural history.

So is religion *merely* cultural? It is important to emphasise the extent to which Williams agrees with Cupitt's 'non-realism'. He too believes that traditional metaphysics is untenable. He does not try to argue that anything such as the afterlife or the soul or indeed God 'really' exists outside of our linguistic practices. But he is a different sort of non-realist, for he wants to affirm these linguistic practices, to stay within them. He wants to preserve the language of God's objective existence, his priority to us, our need of his grace. Cupitt's tendency is to disparage this basic Christian pathos, to suggest that it is unsustainable. Williams wants to share Cupitt's philosophical honesty, but to uphold what is seen through – the 'primary' language of religious assent. Yes, religion is completely and utterly cultural and linguistic – but we must learn to say so with a Christian rather than an Enlightenment accent.

Oxford movement

Williams' years at Cambridge had established him as the young star of Anglican theology. In 1986 he returned to Oxford, where he had been a postgraduate student. Almost exactly ten years after submitting his doctoral thesis, he was offered the Lady Margaret chair in divinity.

Over the next few years, his work was often concerned with the concept of tradition. This emphasis should be related to the debates within the Church of England at this time. In 1987 the Church's division between traditionalists and liberals suddenly exploded. A traditionalist priest called Garry Bennett committed suicide, having accused the Church of secularism in the Crockford's Preface (a high-profile annual essay). There was a period of soul-searching and press analysis. What did the Church of England now stand for?

To traditionalists, the Church seemed to be going with the liberal tide; to be politically left-wing, and doctrinally vague. It seemed part of 'the liberal establishment', and sometimes posed as the unofficial opposition to the government. The Bishop of Durham was of course the figurehead of such an image – some said that Archbishop Runcie was too close to him. In the background of all this was the looming issue of women's ordination. The practice had begun elsewhere in the Anglican Communion, and the debate was becoming central to the Church of England.

Most of the sternest opponents of ordaining women were Anglo-Catholics. Even Anglo-Catholics from the socially radical tradition were very often opposed (most of the Jubilee Group were opposed, for example). It seemed to be the cause of the liberals, who were deemed to lack respect for Catholic tradition. Williams of course felt the force of the conservatives' argument, but in the mid 1980s he came out as a reformer. An old friend was surprised – shocked, even. Williams was, since adolescence, such a connoisseur of liturgical tradition that his backing of this huge and sudden innovation seemed anomalous.

Williams wanted to change the terms of the debate. Dividing the Church between 'traditionalists' and 'liberals' was a terrible hindrance to the Church's self-understanding. His whole theological agenda was, and is, an attempt to show that things are not so simple. For he is an Anglo-Catholic who claims to be orthodox rather than liberal, yet is obviously heavily indebted to theological liberalism. In these years he sought to show that 'tradition' and 'catholicity' were not defunct ideas but could be reaffirmed by means of the very latest thought. True fidelity to the tradition precluded mere traditionalism: 'Nostalgia for a pre-critical world is a pointless and dishonest response to our situation.'[55] His agenda now seemed clearer and more urgent than ever: to wrest Catholic orthodoxy from the die-hard traditionalists, to make it new.

This imaginative approach to tradition is evident in an essay of 1986 entitled 'Trinity and Revelation'. Though Christian revelation is final and complete, Christians are always learning more about how it relates to our world: 'The work continues, for the theologian and the church at large, of discerning and naming the Christ-like events of liberation and humanization in the world as Christ-like, and, at the level of action, expressing this hermeneutical engagement in terms of concrete practical solidarity.'[56] This emphasis upon the church's involvement in a learning process means that the boundaries of the Christian community will always be in question:

> the constant re-learning of Jesus' significance has to do with an honest awareness of the strain and conflict presently experienced in the Church. Problems such as the ordination of women, the revision of the liturgy, the place and function of episcopacy, baptismal policy in secularized areas, and so on, are essential stages in the 'hermeneutical spiral' whereby the significance of Jesus, the divinity (the decisive generative quality) of Jesus, is recovered ... So my thesis is that any such puzzlement over 'what the Church is meant to be' is the revelatory operation of God as 'Spirit' insofar as it keeps the Church engaged in the exploration of what its foundational events signify.[57]

The average Catholic would surely feel rather alarmed by this account. For there is little sense of the intrinsic authority of the institution, or of its traditional practices. Nothing is sacred – except the quest to rediscover the divinity of Jesus. The church seems to be an argument, an experiment, rather than a reliable mediator of God.

Another aspect of his radically cultural approach is evident in an essay of 1987, 'The Nature of a Sacrament'. With reference to Aquinas, Wittgenstein and David Jones, he argues that human culture is at root sacramental; it is based in an endless process of 'sign-making'. The religion of ancient Israel may be understood in this way: 'acts performed under the divine law are "significant" of the God who brought the slaves out of Egypt.'[58] This religion is not confined to a cultic space; it extends to all of culture: 'As sign-makers in the observance of the Law, the whole of Israel is a priestly people.'[59] This is the background to the advent of Christ, who was 'a sign-maker of a disturbingly revolutionary kind'. He signified the new society of the Kingdom of God: 'his acts are signs of a form of human life yet to be realized and standing at odds with the political and cultic status quo.'[60] He thus takes on the whole weight of Israel's signification of God: 'What Torah was, Christ is . . . He proclaims the imperatives of the kingdom, realizes them in his life and death, and so begins to make the possible community actual in the post-Easter experience of his followers.'[61] There is a crucial ambiguity here: does the church realise the Kingdom, or continue to signify it?

He now discusses the sacraments themselves; they should be understood as pieces of human ritual. 'In these acts the Church "makes sense" of itself, as other groups may do, and as individuals do; but its "sense" is seen as dependent on the creative act of God in Christ.'[62] It seems that what goes on in the sacraments is merely human, like any other communal ritual – except that this piece of anthropological data refers to a uniquely significant event:

> the primary concern should be for sacramental actions rather than an attempt to focus on 'sacralized' objects. There is a perfectly respectable theology (which I accept) of devotion to the consecrated eucharistic elements; but to concentrate on the presence of Christ in this way in some near-total abstraction from the context of the eucharistic action is to court the distortions we began by noting – the isolation of the sacrament as a sign of the divine power's capacity to produce a miraculous 'thing'.[63]

This is a good example of how Williams affirms Catholic tradition, but deconstructs it in the process. He sees the sacraments much as an anthropologist does – as human rituals, yet he also wants to uphold the traditional Catholic understanding of their supernatural character. So his high theology of the sacraments, and the church, is transparently founded on a structure (postmodern linguistic anthropology) that would *seem* to undermine it. It is as if he has demonstrated the nakedness of the emperor and then returned to praising his new clothes. My point is that Williams' ecclesiology is *precariously* high.

The birth of church

What is the church meant to be? For Williams, any answer must refer to its origins, to the experience of the first Christian centuries. In the mid-1980s this approach was more prominent than usual, for in these years his primary field of research was Patristics – the period of the early Fathers of the church. In 1987 he published his biggest book so far, *Arius: Heresy and Tradition*.

The Arian heresy is of especial interest for Williams because it provokes the emergence of Christian orthodoxy, the credal core to which almost all churches have since subscribed. It was the achievement of the Council of Nicaea, whose principal theological mastermind was Athanasius. The argument between Athanasius and Arius, Williams suggests, might help us to see beyond the 'sterile dialogue of the deaf that prevails in so much present discussion between doctrinal "conservatives" and "liberals".'[64] And it might cure us of supposing 'that contemporary "right belief" has no connection with or conditioning by a specific past and present.'[65]

Around the time of the Council of Nicaea, the church emerged as a single, coherent institution. This is because Constantine had just converted, and put the weight of the empire behind the church. The church could now make authoritative pronouncements that were actually enforceable. And so it tried to establish right doctrine – orthodoxy. In practice, this was the beginning of an ongoing process, for the church soon discovered that 'continuity was something that had to be re-imagined and recreated at each point of crisis'. The church therefore claims to have the authority to re-interpret God's revelation, to be able to speak God's mind, as it were. And of course this raises the danger of 'ideological distortion':

> Theologically speaking, an appeal to the Church's charter of
> foundation in the saving act of God, rooted in the eternal act
> of God, can never be made without the deepest moral

ambiguities, unless it involves an awareness of the mode of that saving act as intrinsic to its authoritative quality and as requiring its own kind of obedience. That is to say, the God who works in disponibilité, vulnerability and mortality is not to be 'obeyed' by the exercise or the acceptance of an ecclesial authority that pretends to overcome these limits. But this is a refinement not readily to be discerned in Athanasius . . .[66]

So the church's legitimacy depends upon its development of a sort of benign authoritarianism. But why does Christianity need any centralising authority at all? Williams answers this with reference to the nature of the Arian heresy, against which orthodoxy defined itself. Arius had doubted the doctrine of the incarnation: God cannot be limited by such a doctrine, he said. To say that he is fully present in Jesus is to say too much – Arius' style of theology was apophatic, or negative. In condemning him, the Council of Nicaea established the essential logic of the church. It must marginalise other accounts of Christianity, in order to establish the core idea of God's total involvement in humanity – his incarnation. Nicaea therefore associates two things: the doctrine of God's total involvement in the human world, and the church's right to define God. The latter may be seen as an aspect of the former. The authority of the church is an expression of God's full revelation in human culture. He wills to be limited and defined in this way. 'The Nicene faith establishes a "classical" shape for the aspirations of Christian spirituality; and it could be argued too . . . that Nicene Christianity also does something to secure a certain seriousness about the conditions of human history.'[67]

Williams returns to this territory two years later, in an article entitled 'Does it make sense to speak of pre-Nicene orthodoxy?' In its first two centuries the church managed without orthodoxy. 'Paul's reflection on Christ,' for example, 'carries the seeds of wildly divergent theologies.'[68] Yet, even before Nicaea, orthodoxy begins to emerge: Christianity seems to gravitate towards it, Williams claims.

The emergence of Christianity as a coherent religion is its discovery that it cannot be rootless. It cannot simply criticise the existing religious practices of Judaism and paganism; it must develop some of its own. This distinguishes it from Gnosticism, which locates its essence in a supernatural experience known to all true believers. Christianity, by contrast, begins to offer 'a public, a social, identifying context for the believer – institutional, narrative and behavioural norms'.[69] And this serves to link up disparate groups of believers. The concepts of orthodoxy and catholicity are therefore intimately related. But in the pre-Nicene period these concepts entail flexibility: local difference is tolerable.

Orthodoxy curtails this flexibility, with a scriptural canon, and doctrinal regulation. Modern critics often look upon this process with suspicion, as if an oppressive institution is taking over. Instead, says Williams, Christianity is rightly acquiring cultural objectivity. When certain texts are prioritised, and the form of the liturgy is standardised, the 'otherness' of the Christian story becomes assured. It acquires a life of its own, a separateness from every type of adherent. Without its institutional regulation,

> the story loses its distance or difference, and so its converting power, by becoming simply a story I choose to tell myself. It may be that the very nature of the basic Christian narrative carries the notions of canon and orthodoxy within it . . . The 'catholic' insight is that [the believer's relationship to God] continues to be *constituted* by historical mediations – gospel and canon, sacrament, succession, communion, debate and exchange, with all the ambiguities involved in the life of historical and visible social realities, the problems of power and guilt and forgetfulness.[70]

Institutional regulation therefore has the paradoxical effect of opening up Christianity to diversity, debate, development. For Christianity's essence has become cultural, and human culture is always mutable, open to correction. Williams sees this in incarnational and indeed kenotic terms. As he puts it elsewhere:

> the Christian story shows a God who lets himself be spoken of – defined – in terms of the relation between him and creatures, in terms of the human history he sets in motion and shapes. He chooses to be the God of Israel and of Jesus Christ . . . [he engages with his creation] in such a way that we do not and cannot speak of him only as a remote cause, but must 'define' him in and through the lives that struggle to respond to his pressure and presence.[71]

Williams is developing an original postmodern defence of church-based orthodoxy. True catholicity understands God as culturally mediated. He allows himself to be limited by historical institutions, in order to express his absolute involvement in human history. It hardly needs to be said that there are problems with this. Is it really God's purpose to incarnate himself in ecclesiastical orthodoxy – even at the expense of sacralising a human institution? And what about the church's fragmentation – *which* orthodoxy is the carrier of God's objectivity?

Utopian vision?

The breadth and flexibility of Williams' thought is amazing. In *Arius* he is at his most conservative, using postmodernism in defence of ecclesiastical tradition. But at around the same time he often exhibits the radical social vision at the basis of his thought.

In an essay of 1989, he considers an important tradition of Anglican social thought. Following F. D. Maurice in the mid nineteenth century, an 'incarnationalist consensus' began to emerge. It insists that holiness cannot be confined to the 'religious' sphere but permeates society. The family and the nation are – potentially – religious categories. The church should not compete with these structures, but should affirm them. Such thought became popular again in the 1960s, he notes; there was a widespread 'refusal to draw a firm boundary between sacred and secular'.[72]

But in recent years, he observes, theologians have become a bit more cautious about relating the incarnation to society – and with good reason. The church must remember that 'there is a rather fundamental Christian tradition of *not* belonging, in families, nations, patriarchal "organic" states.'[73] It will always call 'natural' social structures into question, or, if it does inhabit them, it will do so uneasily, provisionally. Only so can it preserve its missionary character, its attempt to be relevant to every form of human existence. 'Its relevance to all *depends* on its difference from existing patterns of human relation and power: if it "fulfils" anything, it is a buried capacity for communion between human beings as such.'[74]

He now relates this to Christology. Divinity, for both Jew and pagan, is bound up with the ability to create a new social group. This is what it means to say that Jesus fully reveals God:

> In short, the question of Jesus' status arises out of his role in the formation of a human community different from what we ordinarily think of as 'natural' communities, a community

whose limits are at the same time the ultimate natural 'limits'
– 'the ends of the earth'. *The world we inhabit* is the potential
scope of the community that is created by relation to Jesus. It
is, you might say, a social vision that shapes the doctrine of the
Incarnation, in the first instance, not the reverse; or rather, it is
the social *fact* of a community with no foreordained
boundaries.[75]

It is a commonplace that Christianity overcomes divisions and aims
at human unity – the sort of thing it costs nothing to say. But
Williams goes further, with surprising boldness: *its truth consists in
this*. The creation of a universal society is the whole point. This is
what it means to say that Jesus is divine – this is the criterion of
religious truth.

Because of its commitment to the creation of a universal
society, the church must stand apart 'from all communities and
kinships whose limits fall short of the human race. The Church's
primitive and angular separateness . . . is meant to be a protest on
behalf of a unified world . . . [T]he Church needs practices, con-
ventions and life-patterns that keep alive the distinctiveness of the
Body . . . a church which does not at least possess certain features
of a "sect" cannot act as an agent of transformation.'[76] He relates this
to the question of the Church of England's establishment: it is rooted in the attempt to create a universal society, 'a community without boundaries other than Christ . . . [but] it is doubtful whether
such a situation could speak of unrestricted human community
when it will inevitably be seen as privileging one of a number of
religious groupings within the state.'[77]

His underlying point is that the church must be separatist in
order to be universalist. But the sectarian emphasis should not be
overstated, he insists. It was no bad thing that the church began to
affirm the basic structures of its surrounding culture. 'By the time
of Augustine's *City of God*, there is a complex theory of belonging
in a cosmic order that includes the family and the empire.' The
church must not reject cultural history, but must work with it – for
this religion is intrinsically and consciously cultural; it does not
pretend that we can escape cultural history into a purer realm.

So the church's relationship to society is rather paradoxical, in
Williams' account. It must exist as a distinctive cultural entity, a separate 'sectarian' institution *because of* its pursuit of 'unrestricted

human community'. But this latter point is the bottom line, the criterion of ecclesiology: to herald a 'unified world' is what the church is *for*.

The emphasis is present in another essay of 1989: here he likens the Christian vision to the 'long revolution' envisaged by Trotskyism. It aspires to 'a condition that history is itself (by definition) incapable of realizing – a perfect communality of language and action free from the distortions imposed on understanding by the clash of group interests and the self-defence of the powerful.'[78] The latter ideal is akin to the 'ideal speech situation' envisaged by the philosopher Habermas. 'Being Christian,' he writes the following year, 'is being involved in witness to and work for a comprehensive human community because of what has happened to specific human beings and their relationships in connection with the ministry, cross and resurrection of Jesus.'[79]

Repeatedly in these years Williams emphasises that Christianity enables the creation of a new society that is without boundaries, that can extend to the ends of the earth. As we have seen, he suggests that the divinity of Christ is a matter of his ability to inaugurate and inspire this new society. Let us call this emphasis on unrestricted human community by its proper name. It is utopian. It exalts the humanly impossible ideal of a universal, undivided, peaceful society. But how does the particularity of the church fit in with this?

In another essay of 1990 he relates the histories of the church and Israel. The idea of Judaism is that the God of all humanity can only be manifest in a particular people. Christianity claims to be free of this limitation, to be the herald of a truly universal society: 'but it has commonly offered only an ersatz universality, a large-scale tribalism with Christ as source and guarantor of the authoritative and comprehensive system of meaning purveyed by the Church.'[80] This is an absolutely crucial admission. The church generally *fails* to realise the universality of the Christian vision. For Williams, the solution to this is appropriate humility, especially with regard to Israel. The church must realise that it has a tragically self-contradictory dimension: it is the communicator of universal humanity, yet it seems unable to shirk self-regarding particularity. In a sense its claim to be the new Israel is ironic; it is just more of the same, but it is less honest than Israel, more prone to self-delusion, more pretentious.

The central question, then, is how the society of the church relates to the universal social ideal. Is the church as it actually exists the beginning of this new universal society? Yes, Williams seems to say: the actual Christian community is the means to a universal human society. Yet he also admits that the church *stands in the way* of its core vision, that it tends to see itself as a *replacement* for the Kingdom rather than its humble agent. If the goal of Christianity is the creation of a truly universal society, as Williams repeatedly hints, then surely conventional ecclesiology must be overhauled? This is really *the* question I want to put to Williams. From what we have seen so far, his work repeatedly half-raises it, but backs off, as if there is nothing to be gained from sticking with it. He magisterially assures us that the 'orthodox' church is, for its sins, nevertheless the true site of this universalist vision. This model cannot be improved on. Despite the tragic dimension of church, God wills the show to go on. My whole thesis is that this assurance is *fragile*; it is half-aware of its inadequacy.

CHAPTER THREE

WALES

IN 1991 THE Oxford professor was invited to be Bishop of
Monmouth. He had always been primarily a priest, secondarily
an academic – in theory. In practice he enjoyed the relative freedom of a priest employed as an academic. Might episcopal office
not cramp his theological style? He later remarked on 'the deep
suspicion with which churches habitually regard theologians'.[1] And
the new Archbishop of Canterbury, George Carey, was not quite his
sort of Anglican, to put it politely. On the other hand, he was serv-
ing the Church in Wales, making him less answerable to Carey. This
also made him less implicated in the Church's establishment: the
appointment of Welsh bishops does not involve the Crown.

With Anglican politics hotting up, he knew he might have a
few fights on his hands. Before accepting he wrote a letter to the
archbishop of Wales setting out his views on women's ordination,
homosexuality and peace issues, so that he need not feel
constrained by the mitre from speaking his mind.

Becoming a bishop was obviously a huge practical change. It
meant exchanging the dreaming spires for a view of a slagheap in
Newport, and the occasional seminar for the endless confirmation
class. He later admitted that he missed aspects of academic life, 'But
I still think I am a theologian, and that is my task as a Bishop – to
try to be a teacher and interpreter of the faith.'[2]

Does the move affect his ecclesiology? In particular, does it
make him slower to question conventional ecclesiology, to probe
its limits? To some extent yes: he becomes more conscious that
he speaks in and for the Church – and of course this increases with
his appointment as Archbishop of Wales in 2000 and then his

appointment to Canterbury. 'I have to be as honest as I can within the framework of the responsibilities I have to a large range of people,' he has said recently; 'as Archbishop I have to keep as many voices in play as possible.'[3] This must be a terrible renunciation for an intellectual, one feels. And then one suspects that Williams rather relishes the role of voicing a corporate body, like some sort of episcopal shaman.

So he does not simply repress his ecclesiological radicalism. He attempts to incorporate it into his episcopal role. As a bishop he becomes more intent on nurturing innovation within the church. As we have seen, he has always held that a key part of the bishop's role is looking for fresh opportunities, making connections with the surrounding culture – what might be called 'outreach', or in business jargon, 'research and development'. For example, he insists that a bishop must make attempts to meet young people, 'however difficult and embarrassing'.[4] This emphasis on innovation continues, and indeed increases, when he comes to Canterbury, as we shall see.

Affirming Catholic

Williams joined the Anglican episcopacy in one of the most testing years it had ever known. As we saw, the issue of women's ordination had threatened to split the Church since the mid 1980s. In November 1992 General Synod finally debated women's ordination in earnest, and then passed the Women's Ordination Measure by the necessary two-thirds majority. But it was not an entirely decisive win. Synod subsequently decreed that dissenting congregations could remain fully Anglican, even while rejecting women priests as heretical. The result of this was that communion was 'impaired'. Those parishes rejecting women priests constituted a church within a church. This grouping, Forward in Faith, was of course on the Catholic wing of the Church. It had a reasonable claim to represent the Catholic mainstream, being closer to Roman and Orthodox practice.

Yet most of those calling themselves Anglo-Catholic accepted the ordination of women. In 1990 some of these had formed a new group, Affirming Catholicism. Williams was its vice-president. He articulated its basic insight: tradition should be seen 'not as a lifeboat to escape the present' but as 'a crucible in which the experiment of Christian life is constantly tested'.

In 1991 he wrote a book that might be seen as an oblique contribution to the cause of women's ordination. *Teresa of Avila* is largely about the church's need to adapt to new insights, to open itself to judgement. Teresa's mystical experience was a challenge to ecclesiastical authority: such a tension is inevitable in 'any tradition that is not content to settle simply for ritual and ideology, any tradition concerned to continue the process of discovery and maintaining its integrity.'[5] The church can never relax, never feel that it has got it right.

> Christianity is a faith marked in its very origins by unsettling new perspectives on human unity and equality, on the nature of community and the exercise of power. Studying Teresa reminds us of some of these disturbances built into the Church's story, those awkward and still unresolved challenges to our systems of hierarchy and separation . . . she reminds us that we do not yet know what it would be like if the community of Christ's friends let themselves be fully taken up into God's self-imparting act.[6]

In July 1993 he addressed the launch of the Gloucester branch of Affirming Catholicism, calling for an attitude of confidence rather than defensiveness from Catholic-minded Anglicans. Catholic Christians must not discredit other forms, but must develop 'a sense of complementary vocations'. The existence of other styles can teach us about our shortcomings:

> We can celebrate the Eucharist with drama and dignity, hieratically, impressively, with historic liturgical structures . . . And when we have done all that, we are still unprofitable servants because there is something we have not seen that a Quaker supper or a Brethren meeting breaking bread may say and we cannot say. We can meet that in a spirit of rivalry or suspicion or else in a spirit of gratitude and I want to put in my vote for a spirit of gratitude. That is part of what I mean by a Church both Catholic and Reformed, not eager to reconsolidate a smooth system, and prepared to live with plurality not because it is indifferent, but because it is in fear and trembling of the mysteriousness and richness of God which no system can manage for us . . .[7]

Anglicanism is especially free to understand Catholicism in this way, he suggests. Its institutional untidiness might worry a Roman Catholic, but 'Our method is in the long run more effective, for the mind and the conscience go with it . . .' To be a 'reformed Catholic' 'doesn't mean saying "no" to our heritage but saying "yes" to the full richness of it, the complexity of a tradition that is also capable of bringing itself under judgement, a tradition that is still able to hear a word from outside and to come back to be tested and perhaps sometimes broken on the rock of Christ.' But is such an open-minded account of Catholicism practically sustainable? Does it have enough institutional conservatism?

The same question is raised by a lecture discussing the future of the papacy.[8] He begins by restating the idea that catholicity is related to the faith's *objectivity*, its difference from this or that particular context. The impulse behind papal power is understand-able to an Anglo-Catholic such as himself, but its history seems indefensible: 'from an Anglican, as from an Orthodox point of view, almost everything said theologically about the papacy between 1000 and 1500 is at best outrageous and at worst materially blasphemous.' Although 'the notion of a reliable institutional focus of unity' is attractive, the papacy still entails illegitimate centralisa-tion. This is especially evident in papal visits – they display 'the cult of personality, the pseudo-communality of the large crowd of enthusiasts . . . [and] a collusiveness with the impersonal emotion-alism that makes totalitarianism possible.' Many would argue that Anglican leadership must follow suit, if the Communion is to survive:

> But I'd rather argue that the difficulties of this office simply show the real state of international Christianity: it is culturally varied, and centralising authority increasingly doesn't work, except by doing some violence to local church life (and often not even then). The Anglican situation, about which I have no illusions of grandeur or success, means that the Communion's focus *has no option* but to acknowledge the weakness of the unifying gospel in the face of cultural and political diversity, and to let the hope of the gospel speak from, not against, that acknowledged weakness . . . We have the rather awkward job in our Communion of recognising that our systems of inter-national interpretation and sharing are a mess . . . [Nevertheless] there is a focal and life-giving belief to be

shared, something to which all local communities remain
answerable, and . . . the minister of unity has to serve just this.

The question is whether this 'kenotic' model of leadership is capable of supporting anything resembling an ecclesiastical institution.
What if this non-papal model of leadership ends up 'broken on the
rock of Christ'? Would it matter?

Sacramental anarchist?

Around this time, with the dust unsettled from the ordination of
women, the next big unity-eating issue was emerging: homosexuality. Since the late 1980s Williams had opposed the Church's line
on homosexuality (in 1987 General Synod decreed that sex should
only ever take place within marriage). In 1991 the Church produced a document called *Issues in Human Sexuality*. It said that
priests should not be practising homosexuals, but did not extend
the proscription to laypeople. Williams could not accept its authority; he tried persuading Carey not to approve it. He particularly
objected to the double standard, the distinction made between
priests and laypeople. In 1998 his liberalism on the issue harmed his
prospects of promotion under Carey. He was considered for the
Diocese of Southwark, a job he wanted, but refused to assure Carey
that he would toe the line on homosexuality, and was not offered
the job. In the same year the Lambeth Conference met, and, to
liberal dismay, confirmed the ban on homosexual priests. Williams
did not only voice his dissent, he put it into practice, by ordaining
someone he knew to be homosexual.

Williams was teaching that the Christian approach to sexual
ethics requires a sacramental emphasis. This is the alternative to
legalism, a set of binding rules gleaned from either the Bible or
'natural law':

> What if we start from somewhere else? The gospel is about a
> man who made his entire life a sign that speaks of God and
> who left to his followers the promise that they too could *be*
> signs of God and *make* signs of God because of him. Even in
> this unpromising world, where we are so prone to deceive
> ourselves, things and persons can come to 'mean', to show,
> God's meanings – to communicate the creative generosity and
> compassion which, we learn from revelation, is the most basic

reality there is. In more theological language, Jesus is himself
the first and greatest *sacrament*, and he creates the possibility
of things and persons, acts and places, being in some way
sacramental in the light of what he has done.[9]

He proceeds to argue that sexual fidelity is, in the Christian, a crucial sign of God's commitment. Instead of asking whether we are
obeying the rules, we must ask of our sexual lives, 'How much am
I prepared for this to signify?'[10]

This treatment of sexual ethics has ecclesiological implica-
tions. The Christian must understand his or her life in sacramental
terms — but this sacramentalism is at least semi-detached from the
church; it cannot be ecclesiologically regulated. God is signified by
faithful homosexual union, even if the institutional churches
officially deny this. He is advocating a sort of sacramental
Protestantism, in which no institution can claim to control the
Christian signing of God. We must all work out our own 'sacramental ethics' rather than trust the teachings of the church. Does
this not undermine the church's claim to dispense authoritative
moral teachings?

The homosexuality issue is therefore a glimpse into Williams'
true ecclesiological radicalism. He does not really believe in the
church as an institution empowered to tell us what is morally good.
This whole aspect of the church is an embarrassment — perhaps an
inevitable one, but an embarrassment nevertheless. The true function of the church is not moral direction. It is to stage the central
symbolic drama that interprets all else. As he puts it elsewhere, the
sacraments are 'the steady course run by divine reality in our midst,
the life and death and resurrection of Jesus, into which our lives are
invited, so that they weave in and out of that solid and central
history — and sometimes are so drawn in, woven in, that they
become a kind of sacrament themselves.'[11]

Elsewhere he argues that ethics in the New Testament is not
about rules; it is about the will to communicate God. For Paul, 'the
practice of the ethical life by believers is a communicative strategy,
a discourse of some sort'; and for Matthew, 'ethics is about manifestation . . . Christian virtue is there to display a reality that will
cause thanksgiving and delight, that will cause people to give glory
to the Father.'[12]

It often seems as if Williams wants the church to be nothing but the company that puts on the Eucharist, that he would like to move away from its role as ethical guide. Some might question whether his epiphanic approach to ethics is compatible with church order and unity. Must not a church defend its authority, by presenting a united front on thorny moral questions? Such a view has recently been expressed by George Carey:

> The Church has a very deep responsibility to uphold its historic moral insights and teaching, even while we continue to explore their fullness of meaning and their most adequate contemporary expression. The teachings of the Church are not arbitrary or frivolous, and may not be cast aside with misplaced presumption.[13]

Perhaps this is intended as a rebuke to someone in particular.

Church as postmodern polis

Around 1990, postmodern theology came of age; it moved from the margins to the centre of academic theology. As we have seen, Williams had long been developing an ecclesiology steeped in postmodern thought: from the late 1980s on, this becomes more pronounced, explicit and ambitious. And it also becomes necessary to distance himself from other exponents of postmodern ecclesiology, to warn against certain dubious tendencies. To consider his involvement in these debates it is necessary to step back slightly, and consider the development of postmodern theology during the late 1980s.

As we began to see in Chapter One, postmodern theology is defined by its reaction against the influence of the Enlightenment. Liberal theology had tried to justify itself in terms of universal human reason – the holy grail of modernism. Postmodern theology declares its liberation from this aspiration; it insists that Christianity's truth can only be expounded in the context of a particular community – ecclesiology therefore becomes central. In contrast to postmodernism in general, theological postmodernism has a strongly conservative, perhaps reactionary, character. A new sort of authority is conferred on traditional practices. Despite his fundamental sympathy, Williams was aware of the danger in this tendency: had he helped to spawn a highly sophisticated form of fundamentalism?

During the mid 1980s a fairly coherent school of postmodern theology emerged in America, known as the 'postliberal' school. It combined Wittgenstein's 'socio-linguistic' thought with Barth's rejection of theological liberalism. It was also informed by new readings of Aristotle, especially his emphasis on the *community* as the site of moral value. In this view, goodness and truth are not abstract, objective things but are situated in the narrative that a particular community tells about itself, and lives out. Williams was somewhat influenced by these thinkers, but he continued to feel closer to the Roman Catholic theologians we have already noted, above all Nicholas Lash and Fergus Kerr.

Williams might be seen as the political conscience of post-modern theology: he was intent on translating his political radical-ism into this new idiom, and wary of an anti-historical impulse in some forms of postmodern thought. This is evident in an essay on Augustine's *City of God* that made the fifth-century theologian seem a fellow postmodern. It argues that Augustine should not be read as anti-political, an advocate of otherworldliness. His aim was to expose the inadequacy of a merely secular vision, such as the Roman empire embodied, and thus to create a new sort of politi-cal discourse. 'Augustine does not think . . . of two distinct kinds of human association, the sacred and the secular, or even the private and the public . . . [he] seeks to show that the spiritual is the *authen-tically* political. At the end of the day, it is the secular order that will be shown to be "atomistic" in its foundations.'[14] Because Rome is based on violence and elitism, it cannot be a true commonwealth, a good society in the fullest sense. Its ideology of justice and so on is always pretentious: 'classical society and classical political thought provide ideals for the corporate life of humanity which they cannot provide the means to realise.'[15] The city of God, the church, should not be seen as an escape from the political but as a critique of the failure of secular politics. By establishing a community of *caritas* (charity, peace) it shows what the political realm could be. This function is fully *political*: this other society exists in the *polis* and exerts a crucial influence.

For Williams then, Augustine does not reject politics in favour of religion but overcomes the distinction – *The City of God* 'is not at all a work of political theory in the usual sense, but sketches for a theological anthropology and a corporate spirituality.'[16] The church develops a more serious and comprehensive account of politics, one that is not limited by the contingent perspective of any particular *polis*. All other accounts of the political good are locked in violent, dehumanising patterns. Only this utterly novel political vision can pursue true justice rather than settle for a pragmatic, compromised, self-interested version.

In a sense the church pursues an *unrealistic* political vision, in that it cannot be directly realised by any actual state. For in practice the state must defend itself, prefer the contingent good to the absolute good. Yet this unrealistic vision is also realistic, for it knows that it cannot be immediately realised; it resists the chiliastic, or utopian, impulse. Elsewhere, he touches on this paradox in relation to the philosopher Simone Weil. She rejects Tolstoyan pacifism, says Williams, because 'she is not naïve enough to think that the social structure can do without coercion. Her concern, however, is the ease with which we persuade ourselves that the relationships constituted by force are *normative*.'[17] One must resist the 'realistic' worldview that violence is the most basic reality, that the world is essentially chaotic, and affirm instead that the world is essentially good, originally and ultimately peaceful. Yet one must accept that a non-violent politics cannot be engineered; it can only be anticipated, symbolised, witnessed to.

Violence, myth and ritual

The intrinsic violence of secular politics is an important theme in Williams' thought: we understand the church by seeing how it exposes this and offers an alternative. Here he is influenced by various thinkers, including Augustine as we have just seen, but one of the most prominent is the French Roman Catholic anthropologist René Girard. According to Girard, competitive violence is natural to human culture. Primitive religion is a response to this; it channels this latent violence in the sacrifice of an arbitrary scapegoat, and so restores peace. But Christianity, says Girard, is different: it confronts this dynamic rather than appeasing it; it offers an alternative social myth, about the rejection of rivalry and exclusion. Since the late 1980s, Williams became increasingly attracted to Girard's thought, and it was no fleeting interest. In a controversial sermon of 2004, touching on the Iraq war, he warned of 'those habits of acquisitive rivalry that dominate our relations and breed our conflicts. As René Girard has reminded us, we learn from each other to want what the other wants, and so to compete with the other for its possession . . .'[18]

In a lecture on Girard he notes that no comprehensive theological position emerges from his thesis. Though he presents Christ as the unmasker of sacred violence, he gives us little sense of how a new tradition emerges, 'of how a community founded on the *overthrow* of sacred violence actually develops and works.'[19] His approach is abstract, theoretical – he does not ground his discourse 'in the realised possibility of a corporate human life free of victimage, the gift of non-violent relation'.[20] He seems to question the ability of the church to express the Gospel of non-violence:

> [He is] not simply advocating a return to ecclesiastical Christianity *sans phrase*. He has no illusions about the degree to which Christianity has colluded with sacrificial violence and found ways of intensifying it. Yet he seems to be saying that a purely secular (in the usual sense of the word) social order is inconceivable . . . We are returned constantly to the necessity of a myth of victimage and its overcoming, a myth against myths. [And we are returned] to the need for a ritual against ritual; and so to the significance of the community created, founded, by the 'anti-sacrifice' of Jesus . . . This community is pretty consistently a travesty of what it is meant to be, but without its *enactment* of the anti-sacrificial text of the gospels in baptism and eucharist, the text remains a piece of information rather than a transforming discovery.[21]

If Girard's thesis is right, he concludes, 'society will continue to stand in need of a community that offers an alternative foundational myth to that of sacred violence.'[22] Williams here seems to present church as an anthropological necessity: this community is the alternative to our violent primal habits, their deconstruction. But is it in practice? Williams characteristically privileges the sacraments as the locus of pure opposition to violence, and admits that the church as a social organisation betrays the vision. But elsewhere he seems to claim that church is an effective society of peace. As he puts it in 2001: 'What we must learn is how to live fraternally with human beings . . . This is precisely what Jesus once and for all makes possible by his teaching, his death and his resurrection. This is the Gospel, this is what the sacraments enact.'[23] Alternatively, this is how he puts it in 2004: 'We cannot turn [our relationship to God] into a matter for competition. Our Christian obedience becomes the foundation for a radically fresh vision of one another. By looking to each other to learn Christ, by looking at another's looking to Jesus, our desires are re-formed and liberated for life in communion.'[24] It's a cheap shot, perhaps, but as he was saying this his flock was violently feuding over homosexuality.

No sects please, we're Catholic

Following Augustine, Williams wants to depict the church as a new sort of political reality – but what does this mean in practice? In one lecture he insists that it is *not* a matter of resacralising the modern state – this would be 'a radical and disastrous misunderstanding of the problem'.[25] Yet on the other hand the church must contest the logic of the secular state, which knows no good beyond its own security and short-term material advantage. All forms of traditional religion challenge this: 'any religious practice symbolising optimal forms of human community or belonging will be tacitly at odds with a secular environment.'[26]

To preserve its capacity to challenge, the church must keep its distance from the existing structures of society, and from any reforming social vision: 'the Christian Church believes itself to be the sign and foretaste of what human society must be, and so cannot arrive at a concordat with some other polity into which elements of Christian morality may be introduced.'[27] This does not mean that the church should isolate itself from its social context, but its primary mode of engagement is simply to be a model of the good society. 'In short, the Church doesn't tell you about the "spirit" in which you ought to conduct the business of the state, but about the pattern of virtues (tangible structures of behaviour, not attitudes alone) characterising the *polis* of God.'[28] This suggests that the church is a mini-society, a purer *polis* within the *polis*. He at once balances this impression by emphasising that the church is an open, messy tradition: 'Its history is one in which critical discontinuities (the Reformation, the Enlightenment . . .) work against the belief that an optimal form of administration and articulation have been attained. Despite perennial pressures, internal and external, in the opposite direction, it has remained a "conversational" phenomenon.'[29] Yet it is not too vague to count: it is 'an active political phenomenon with particular virtues grounded in a particular

commitment . . . [A]s long as there is such a community, however
muddled it may be about how to articulate all this, the contribution, the challenge I've been trying to characterise will not go
away.'[30]

Williams is walking a tightrope here. The proper business of
the church is to be the *polis* of God, he insists – a society within
society that calls secularism to account. Yet this society must not
conceive of itself as a neatly separate, coherent entity. This seems
contradictory: the church must be a distinctive body that lacks clear
definition. Perhaps it takes a leap of faith to square this circle.

The same warning not to define church too closely is made in
his discussion of George Lindbeck, one of the American 'postliberal' school. Lindbeck had urged Christians to live within
the Christian 'text', to interpret the world in terms of the biblical
story: 'to become religious involves becoming skilled in the language,
the symbol system of a given religion. To become a Christian
involves learning the story of Israel and of Jesus well enough to
interpret and experience oneself and one's world in its terms.'[31]

Lindbeck's vision is too tidy, says Williams. In practice, the
boundary between Christian and secular is hugely blurred in modern times. He uses as an example the war poetry of Wilfred Owen
that sometimes uses Christian imagery to indict the failure of
European Christendom. This relates the world to the scriptural
text, but hardly in Lindbeck's way: Owen's purpose is secular rather
than Christian. Williams' point is that the church can learn crucial
lessons from such writers. If it is attentive, 'the Christian community is itself enlarged in understanding and even in some sense
evangelized.'[32] The secular world's reaction to the Christian text can
thus serve to redefine the church's mission; to educate the church
toward maturity.

Williams pursues this argument with surprising radicalism. He
contests the assumption that the church has the definitive worldview which it ought to assert against all others. In reality it has as
much to learn as to teach. 'Words like "preaching" and "interpretation" have come to sound rather weak; or, at least, they do not very
fully characterize the enterprise to which the Church is committed. The Church exists for the sake of the Kingdom of God . . .'[33]
By attending to the concerns of the world with real openness,
rather than trying to bash it with the Gospel, we can move to a
fuller understanding of our calling. 'Can we so *rediscover* our own

foundational story in the acts and hopes of others that we ourselves are reconverted and are also able to bring those acts and hopes in relation with Christ for their fulfilment by the re-creating grace of God?'[34]

This questioning of the adequacy of 'religion' sounds like Bonhoeffer. Indeed he now quotes Bonhoeffer on the sheer ineffectiveness of the church's language, and the need for something new. Williams seems to agree that the conventional apparatus of religion fails to communicate the Gospel to our culture. The church cannot solve its communication failure by being more assertive: it ought patiently to seek 'the expansion of the Christian imagination itself into something that can cope with the seriousness of the world.'[35] This essay is a good illustration of Williams' theological flexibility and freedom: just as a 'postmodern' consensus was forming, a consensus that he had helped to establish – he questions it. Maybe, he says, this new theological paradigm contains reactionary timidity as well as salutary boldness.

A pugnacious pupil

In the early 1990s, one of Williams' former pupils suddenly became a star of postmodern theology. John Milbank had been taught by Williams at Cambridge in the 1980s. He too was an Anglo-Catholic who identified with the politically radical wing of that tradition. Besides Williams, he was influenced by the American postliberals, especially Stanley Hauerwas, who interpreted the church along Aristotelean lines: as a *polis*, a character-forming society – but with little of the reticence and ambiguity we have just discussed in Williams (instead Hauerwas has a sort of cowboy directness – the theological equivalent of George W. Bush, perhaps). Milbank began to develop this insight, helped by Williams' reading of Augustine. He also highlighted Nietzsche's insight that secular liberalism was at root nihilistic, its 'values' were masks for power-bids – an insight developed by thinkers such as Foucault.

Milbank's book of 1990, *Theology and Social Theory: Beyond Secular Reason*, was notably ambitious, polemical, bold. Its introduction announces that modern theology has been timidly subservient to liberal sociology. The point of theology is to 'provide its own account of the final causes at work in human history, on the basis of its own particular, and historically specific faith.'[36] For Milbank, the church embodies the Christian social vision of peace rather than conflict; its practice is 'the imagination in action of a peaceful, reconciled social order' – and this practice is the only real alternative to nihilism.[37]

The debt to Williams ought to be obvious. For Catholic orthodoxy is understood in cultural terms, as the form of life uniquely conducive to social peace. The church is a unique piece of human culture, rooted in certain rituals, and it entails a uniquely affirmative political vision – of all conflicting interests reconciled. In a sense, Milbank is turning Williams' thought into a systematic thesis, assertively delivered. Consequently, to read Williams' response to Milbank, which appeared in 1992, is like watching a man looking at himself in a (slightly distorting) mirror. He sets out his basic query at the beginning: 'is Milbank's commitment to history and narrative, to time as the medium of benign creativity and non-competitive difference, fully realized in his exposition?'[38]

He paraphrases Milbank's thesis thus: 'The Church witnesses to a community without dominion, bonded by charity and forgiveness rather than law, ethnically unrestricted: in this definition of its ideal self, it uncovers what other orders characteristically lack.'[39] The driving force of Christian history is this vision of 'total peace'; it is 'a culture of corporate virtue, instead of competing heroisms, of difference without menace, and of forgiveness'.[40] He notes the impressive force of Milbank's 'insistence on thinking Christ in inseparable relation with the Church' and his 'recovery of a genuinely Augustinian political ethic, the virtues of God's *polis*'.[41] But now he raises his key question: how are we to understand this vision of 'total peace'? 'It seems that we are . . . confronted with something "achieved", and left with little account of how it is learned, negotiated, betrayed, inched forward, discerned and risked.'[42] In other words, this account of church risks claiming too much for the actual phenomenon, and evading the ongoing crisis of church, its addiction to failure, its inability to be the Kingdom of God.

> If our salvation is cultural (historical, linguistic, etc.), it is not a return to primordial harmonics, purely innocent difference . . . [T]he Church's peace is a healed history, not a 'total harmony' whose constructed (and thus scarred) character doesn't show . . . [T]he peace of the Church as an historical community is always in construction.[43]

Milbank's ecclesiology risks triumphalism – he almost forgets that the church is implicated in fallen human history, and is unable to put its vision of total peace into political practice. He is in danger of putting the church on a pedestal, and of setting it 'too dramatically apart from the temporal ways in which the good is realized in a genuinely contingent world.'[44] Theology ought to be more honest about the errors of church history, and present-day problems:'The imagining of "total peace" must somehow be accessible to those whose history is not yet healed or even heard in and by the Church (how might a woman tell this story as a story of peace or promise?).'[45]

Williams is detecting in Milbank something of what he detected in Lindbeck: an urge to express things too neatly, and also too assertively. This is partly a matter of tone: the defiant rejection of 'liberalism' gives the impression that the church has little or nothing to learn from the world around it. A sort of fundamentalism lurks.

Many levelled this charge at Milbank's book – and also at the movement based in his work, Radical Orthodoxy. Williams did not join his name to this movement, but he was the principal teacher of its key founders: its godfather figure. He has subsequently restated his ambivalence. He is sympathetic to the affirmation of classical orthodox doctrine, and especially the emphasis on creation as essentially good rather than essentially fallen.

> My reservation about Radical Orthodoxy . . . concerns the tragic. Granted that violence isn't primary, it might still be going a bit far and too fast to say the church within history achieves the peace it speaks of . . . I think it's important to emphasise that the brokenness, the woundedness of the Christian body in history, at every level, just doesn't go away.[46]

Yet it seems likely that Williams was influenced, or emboldened, by the success of this movement to develop the *anti-secular* accent within his own thought. As we shall see, the theme was very prominent during his first year as Archbishop of Canterbury.

Hegel contra Derrida

During the 1980s another strain of postmodern theology emerged; one that resembles a weird form of gnosticism, a rarefied code-language with spiritual pretensions. We are talking about theo-logical responses to the work of Derrida. 'Deconstruction' is a sort of post-metaphysical philosophy that looks more like literary criti-cism. Its basic agenda is to show that modern thought remains infected by a desire for transcendence, or 'presence'. Even discourse that is secular and rational is metaphysically pretentious – indeed it seems that language itself gravitates towards promising a higher sort of truth than it can deliver. Every statement entails a claim to final-ity, or 'totality'; it suppresses another perspective that calls it into question. The task of thought is always to expose this, to disillusion us. Deconstruction is essentially a technique for undermining any theoretical tidiness or grandeur, showing that every account of truth is, on close inspection, unsure of itself, haunted by what it excludes. (I suppose that we are applying 'deconstruction' to Rowan Williams' ecclesiology.)

How does this affect theology? It sounds like just another vari-ant of secular suspicion. If all meaning is a matter of linguistic con-struction, then we are surely in the realms of Don Cupitt's 'non-realism'. But deconstruction also calls atheism and humanism into question: perhaps these discourses are even more metaphysi-cally pretentious than traditional religious ones, because less aware of their own presumptuous character. Are we then left with nihilis-tic relativism, as if every constructive use of language is equally deluded? Or is there something more positive going on?

Derrida himself (a Jew with an interest in Christian theology) realised that his project was oddly similar to that of certain mysti-cal ('negative') theologians. To approach language with suspicion, as if it is a factory of idolatry, is to assume that there is something that is not idolatry. In 1985 he suggested that deconstruction might be of use in theology:

> [It might help to] liberate theology from what has been graft-ed on to it, to free it from its metaphysico-philosophical super-ego, so as to uncover an authenticity of the 'gospel' . . . [It might be useful] when what needs to be criticized is a whole theological institution which supposedly has covered over, dissimulated an authentic Christian message. [It might enable] a faith lived in a venturous, dangerous, free way.[47]

This suspicion of the 'institution' is significant: Derrida has often made it clear that he is opposed to official religious systems – they necessarily do violence to the elusiveness of God (a similar conclusion to that arrived at by Simone Weil).

In an essay of 1992 Williams acknowledged Derrida as a critical resource: he 'helps us to look warily at systematic claims to overcome the plural and conflictual character of our speech and world'.[48] Yet he also warned that such thought was fascinated (in a negative sense – hypnotised) by the elusiveness of meaning; it involves 'a sacralizing of absence and inception at the expense of the work of social meaning'.[49] Deconstruction can be an excuse to ignore the social project at the heart of modern thought, a quietist detour.

His response to Derrida owes a great deal to the philosopher Gillian Rose. In an essay on her thought he agrees that postmodern theorists are too wary of social thought, which they write off as intrinsically violent. Rose and Williams want to return to Hegel: the Absolute is a dynamic within history. History and metaphysics must be held together. But doesn't this mean absolutising some historical agent such as the church, or Enlightenment rationality? Not necessarily, says Williams, for in the Judeo-Christian narrative God reveals himself indirectly; through a particular human community:

> the paradoxical reality of a community believing itself to stand for the 'interest' of a God without interest or favouritism is somewhere near the centre of how reflective Judaism and reflective Christianity have tried to imagine themselves. As Gillian Rose sees so clearly, the temptation for both is to lose the paradox – and so to lose the political vocation implicit in the paradox, the task of realizing a corporate life whose critical practice constantly challenges sectional interest and proprietorial models of power or knowledge.[50]

In a lecture of 1994 he warns that postmodern pluralism brings 'the prospect of a world in which there aren't and couldn't be real discussions of the goals and destiny of human beings as such.'[51] A common human project becomes harder to speak about. To help us out of this we must look again at the thought of Hegel:

> His conviction was that the supreme political goal was a condition where the individual, in full freedom and integrity, recognized that her or his welfare and purposes could only be understood and realized in and through the welfare and

purposes of the entire community . . . The price of pluralism, certainly in its postmodern varieties, is that such a political vision becomes meaningless.[52]

The church proclaims a universal social vision, which, 'in a society like ours, in a pluralist and privatized environment, is a strange and rather subversive thing to be doing. The practice of mission takes it for granted that it is possible to imagine a community in which the good of each is inseparable from the good of all.'[53] But this universalism must be accompanied by an awareness of 'the dangers of reducing that vision to the claim of an institution whose record is at best uneven, and which constantly slips into treating *itself* as one community among others that must struggle to establish its power or supremacy over others.'[54]

     The way forward is to pursue the universal social vision more fully, and more reflectively: the church must be 'challenged to define itself in such a way that its continuity with a global hope can appear.'[55] But is it really possible for the church to remember its own provisionality, its subservience to the social ideal? Williams explains that the sacraments ought to remind the church that it is never in possession of divine grace, but always stands in need of it. They demonstrate 'our awareness of how we have not mastered [Jesus] and never shall, since it is always he who continues to invite, in the pulpit or at the table or at the font.'[56] He makes the same point in an essay of 1996, in relation to the story of the empty tomb. It ought to remind the church that it cannot claim to possess Jesus. The task of the priesthood is to 'remind the community of the danger of swallowing Jesus up in its own life and practice . . . Ideally, the fact that ordained ministry operates with sacramental symbols designed to emphasise the presence of Jesus in its own proper difference ought to be a safeguard against the rampant ideologizing of clerical power. To say that this is not always how it has worked is an understatement of epic dimensions.'[57] It is difficult to see how Williams avoids the charge of idealising ecclesiastical authority, even as he tries to subject it to criticism. Does he really believe that renewed emphasis on Christ's agency in the sacraments can help to *diminish* the 'ideologizing of clerical power'?

     In another lecture he explains that the doctrine of the Trinity shows God to be intrinsically social. It follows that Jesus' mission is directed at 'unrestricted communion' – he subverts our natural human competitiveness. This means in practice 'a Church constantly chafing at its historical limits and failures, drawn towards the universality of communion it celebrates and proclaims in its Eucharist.'[58] It is 'a community whose sole rationale is the breaking down of partitions. The actual life of any given Christian community will be, no doubt, shot through with division and fear, yet whenever it reminds itself of what it is, in the celebration of Word and sacrament, it makes a statement about its horizon.'[59]

Although the church is 'perennially conscripted into the service of division and corrupted by its own exclusiveness',[60] we are meant to see the glass as half full rather than half empty: the aspiration to total community *has* become possible. 'Jesus' activity gives the reality of a new "way of being in the world", it effects the restoring of community . . . We are authorised to transmit or embody God's longing for life in communion here as a reflection of the perfect mutuality of the divine life in eternity ("Thy kingdom come, on earth as it is in heaven").'[61] Authentic mission, he concludes, will foster the divine aim of unrestricted communion, it will be 'in love with the kingdom'.[62]

A few years later he returns to Hegel's vision: its faith that the good of each individual interest is dependent on the universal good is an expression of trinitarian doctrine:

[This is] the life pointed to by the Christian Church, but conspicuously not realized in its history, since it has been historically guilty of reverting to pre-conscious patterns of power . . . The Church itself has failed in its trinitarian witness, remaining at the historical point of Jesus's collision with the power of his day: it treats freedom as interior and spiritual, and so offers no reconciliation with the political; it does not understand its own belief in the resurrection and the Holy Spirit.[63]

Hegel's basic theological insight is that the ideal human society is 'adumbrated but not realized by the Church'. He recalls us to a form of theology that is intrinsically political, that is 'a way of thinking the nature of human sociality'.[64] But it is questionable whether Williams really grapples with the crisis of ecclesiological particularity that arises from an attempted updating of Hegel.

Should all theologians be committed to an institution?

In an essay of 1995 Williams discusses Michael Ramsey's book of 1936, *The Gospel and the Catholic Church*, which we have already identified as an early influence. Ramsey was learning from Roman Catholicism and Orthodoxy to see the church as an 'epiphany', or manifestation, of God:

> what matters about the Church is not a system of ideas as such (though doctrine and dogma have their place) nor the structure of an organization competent to deliver authoritative judgements and to require obedience (though order is important in its proper context), but what the bare fact of the Church *shows* . . . Fundamentally . . . the Church *is* the message.[65]

There is a danger in this of an ecclesiological fundamentalism, Williams notes; a church could use this idea to put itself beyond criticism. Such an ecclesiology must be rooted in the Eucharist, he explains, with reference to the Greek Orthodox theologian John Zizioulas' book *Being as Communion*, whose epiphanic emphasis is very close to Ramsey's. But still Williams worries that such thought will lend itself to an uncritically conservative interpretation:

> If you begin by taking for granted the historic community, liturgy and hierarchy of the Church, if this is to be the context and the test for all theological utterance, are we not faced with the danger that theology becomes the self-justification of the Church, an ideology of ecclesiastical power? The account of the role of bishops in the Church, for instance, is eloquent and even compelling in terms of epiphany and symbolism; but we must surely also be aware of what it means and has always meant in terms of the concrete exercise of power.[66]

The modern theologian, Williams continues, is obliged to be critical in a way that Ramsey is not – and he hurries to excuse him: 'he was, of course, writing at a time when this particular kind of ideological suspiciousness was by no means a regular part of the intellectual historian's equipment.'[67] (Really? Were not Marx, Nietzsche and Freud common currency in 1936?) Yet today's theologian is at risk of being *merely* critical, he now insists:

If the theologies that emerge from the experience of the victimised and excluded, the theologies that deploy suspicion and ideological critique, are to be in any sense *theology*, not just an expression of an assortment of resentments, they are bound to work with a governing critical model of what the Body might be. They become a manifestation of the life of the Body as a *thinking* life to the extent that they continue to pose as the ultimate critical point of reference a system of relations between persons established by the events of revelation – that is, by the history of Israel and Jesus. Without this, a purportedly critical theology can become an uncritical deployment of whatever are supposed to be the most obvious and socially accessible models of the good life at any given time.[68]

Is he saying that authentic theology will belong to the church? Not quite: authenticity is not a matter of submitting to an institution's authority, but of acknowledging the authority of 'a system of relations between persons established by the events of revelation'. But in practice, he now explains, this 'system of relations' is manifested in 'the sacramental life of the eucharistic assembly'. So the church *is* the necessary context of theology? Instead of simply insisting upon this he again supplies a caveat. There are times when the church has to be redirected 'by history itself, by moments of rupture and protest. But *if* the church has actually been paying attention to the substance of its sacramental life, it ought to be able to interpret such historical moments correctly, and so to "learn in humiliation".'[69]

Williams is trying to avoid presenting the church as a closed circle, to which theology is either loyal or not. He is constructing a semi-permeable hermeneutical circle. We cannot know what the church ought to be, except through experiencing what, in the Eucharist, it is. But sometimes the church misses the point of its own core symbol and needs to be taught by outside forces. But it only knows how to learn rightly from outside if it is already familiar with the normal manifestation of Christian reality, which is intra-ecclesial.

But basically he agrees with Ramsey that the theologian must help to direct the church from within: 'a theology without anchorage in the showing of God's life that is the Church's liturgy becomes uncritical . . . talkative and bold in its own sophistications.'[70] He is claiming to stick with Ramsey's model and to import a higher level of critical acuity. But in reality the model is broken by the introduction of a criterion by which sacramental practice may be judged, an essence that the Eucharist aspires to express. This is a new form of human interrelation – 'a system of relations between persons established by the events of revelation'; 'a remaking of human bonds'. In Williams' account, the church ought to be constantly challenged: does it serve the vision of humanity renewed? As we have previously remarked, there is a sort of Protestantism within his Catholicism, in that he attempts to articulate a principle by which the church's authenticity may be tested.

Loyal realist

In 1997 he returned to the 'non-realist' debate. His position has not changed since his response to Cupitt twelve years back, but its expression has a new dimension now that he is a bishop. There had recently been a controversy surrounding the penalisation of a non-realist vicar; in the light of this he admits that his defence of realism might have a political dimension: 'Realism can act as a means of legitimizing the power of the Church's hierarchy. Anything written on this subject by a bishop is automatically and rightly suspect.'[71] On the other hand, non-realism may also have a political agenda, he suggests. He concludes: 'I still fail to see how what the non-realist advocates can be compatible in the long run with what I understand to be Christian belief. That failure may be hierarchical nervousness or intellectual cowardice; but I hope not.'[72]

The following year he rejects non-realism in more forthright, less apologetic, terms. Bishop John Spong of the Episcopal Church had posted some theses on the internet, demanding a new reformation, in a non-realist direction. Williams reacted with uncharacteristic sharpness. An 'intelligent sixth former' sees doctrinal tradition as bankrupt; but plenty of intelligent adults see it as a 'strange, radically different and imaginatively demanding world that might be inhabited'.[73] Spong overlooks decades, indeed centuries, of hard theological thinking about these issues and his positive proposal amounts to 'a painful example of the sheerly sentimental use of phraseology whose rationale depends on a theology that is being overtly rejected. What can it be more than a rather unfairly freighted and emotive substitute for some kind of bland egalitarianism –

bland because ungrounded and therefore desperately vulnerable
to corruption, or defeat at the hands of a more robust ideology?
It is impossible to think too often of the collapse of liberalism
in 1930s Germany.' The last point is a clear allusion to Karl Barth's
magisterial anti-liberalism.

In his conclusion he returns to the charge of blandness:
Spong's theology of human affirmation entails 'no adoption into
intimate relation with the Source of all; no Holy Spirit. No terror.
No tears.' In reality, the religious affirmation of humanity comes
from 'an immersion in the dark reality of God's difference and in
the uncompromising paradoxes of [the] incarnation of the
Almighty.' The rhetoric here is again Barthian – perhaps even
Kierkegaardian. In the end Spong is guilty of impatience: he wants
to communicate the Gospel to those who assume it is discredited
by modern thought, and hurries to write off the richness of the
tradition. And now Williams admits that this iconoclastic impulse is
not entirely unknown to him:

> Living in the Christian institution isn't particularly easy. It is
> generally, today, an anxious, inefficient, pompous, evasive body.
> If you hold office in it you become more and more conscious
> of what it's doing to your soul. Think of what Coca-Cola does
> to your teeth. Why bother? Well, because of the unwelcome
> conviction that it somehow tells the welcome truth about
> God, above all in its worship and sacraments. I don't think I
> could put up with it for five minutes if I didn't believe this.

Spong's response was to question Williams' motives. He noted that
his promotion to the Diocese of Southwark had just been blocked
by his reputation for liberalism. By reacting so scornfully against a
liberal (on homosexuality as well as doctrine), is he not seeking to
regain Evangelical favour, to 'deliberalise' himself? This is a bit simplistic, as well as a bit ungracious. In reality Williams is committed
to the church (despite his dissent on one ethical question), and he
sees the upholding of doctrinal realism as an essential part of this.
The error of the non-realists is not philosophical; it is ecclesiological. The non-realist is unrealistic about church, about its reliance
on a certain amount of doctrinal realism. For Williams, the non-
realists are putting their own intellectual purity before their duty to
the common endeavour of church. Rattled by Spong's simplistic
and self-righteous position, he reveals more clearly than ever his

discomfort with this, his resentment at the constraint it brings. This is not to say that he is 'really' a non-realist but thinks it his duty to pretend otherwise. Instead he is simply aware of the difficulty involved in his commitment to the church and its teaching.

One senses that Williams dislikes acting as doctrinal police-man, just as he dislikes acting as moral policeman (to the point of refusing to do it as the Church requires). He dislikes his own col-lusion in the uniformity-enforcement aspect of church. As he puts it in 2001, 'Christianity is simply the tradition of speech and prac-tice that transmits the question of Jesus; this is what the Church serves, nothing less and nothing else. It is to this that the Church answers, not primarily to considerations about doctrinal accuracy or institutional coherence.'[74] Its true purpose is obscured by 'neu-rotic efforts at control'. We saw the same thing in his essay on Michael Ramsey: doctrinal and moral order are not the point of the church, but they seem to be (regrettably) necessary concerns — part of the means to the end of an effectively epiphanic church. The end justifies the means.

Lost church?

Lost Icons: Reflections on Cultural Bereavement (2000) is ostensibly the least theological of Williams' books. It is a critique of contemporary culture in which theological categories, including the church, are almost entirely absent. Yet I suggest that a close reading reveals a new perspective on his half-repressed ecclesiological radicalism.

He is using the word 'icons' in an innovative way, he explains: they are 'structures for seeing and connecting in the light of some-thing other than our decisions, individual or corporate'.[75] These old structures have been subjected to intense criticism throughout modernity — as irrational, arbitrary, oppressive. This has resulted in a massive confusion of values, within which a dual danger lurks: the loss of an authentic idea of society, and the loss of the idea of the soul. These two losses are ultimately one. This is really his core argu-ment: the soul needs certain cultural structures, and such structures constitute the 'language of the soul'. Secular discourse seems unable to provide such a language, yet on the other hand 'it is religious language that has borne most of the responsibility for keeping alive of the story of a substantial soul that can live apart from the body and its history'.[76] In other words, the whole concept of the soul needs reinvention in cultural-historical terms, away from its 'otherworldly' aura.

The first chapters analyse the predominance of a social narrative of 'conflict and rivalry'. The antidote is 'charity', understood in its late-medieval sense: the sum of social bonds that knitted society together. Charity is 'the social miracle', the process by which immediate interests are sacrificed for the greater good, the sense 'of belonging with an entire social body extending far beyond one's choice or one's affiliations of interest and "natural loyalty"'.[77] On feast days such as Corpus Christi, 'the public renunciation or transcendence of violent rivalry was more or less obligatory'.[78] In the case of Corpus Christi, of course, the 'social miracle' is explicitly rooted in the theology of the Eucharist and of the church as the body of Christ. Such events had an aura of 'carnival': they allowed different groups to put aside their differences and celebrate their common life in the form of play. Today, Williams argues, the overcoming of factional interest has become impossible; the consumer society is dominant over every other social narrative. 'The idea of a rhythm that controls competition by subversive egalitarian rituals becomes more and more inaccessible; sport becomes another tribal engagement.'[79] Erosion of charity leads to 'fewer controls on rivalry, fewer qualifications to the picture of social life as essentially or primarily conflictual'.[80]

Williams now considers the monarchy as a potential 'icon', in his sense: 'In a rather curious way, monarchy can act and sometimes has acted as a focus for "charity", a ceremonial representation of social cohesion, allowing citizens to find at least a form of lateral equality as "subjects".'[81] This has always been deeply ambiguous, for the obvious reason that the monarch also exercises, or at least symbolises, political power. But now the unifying role of monarchy seems to have gone: 'in a basically secular environment there is no easy way back to the model of the monarch as representing the sacred, the unquestionably "given" in human affairs, the monarch as speaking for a society through the performance of symbolic acts or the receiving of sacral honours.'[82] He suggests that the public reaction to the death of Diana, Princess of Wales represented a wider mourning 'for a whole mythology of social cohesion around anointed authority and mystery'.[83]

In relation to the monarchy Williams acknowledges that the idea of charity was always ambiguous. So how real was 'charity' in any form? He tacitly admits that this is a good question: at one point he makes the provocative statement: 'Charity has evaporated; or else we have recognised that it was never really there.'[84] Surely we need to establish which. If the latter, he is surely open to the dual charge of indulging in nostalgia and neglecting the necessity of modern 'iconoclasm'.

Williams now discusses the shortcomings of the liberal state: social cohesion recedes and the clamour for rights intensifies. Is there an alternative? 'If we could imagine a political system that was more than liberal, it would have to be one that actively supported or promoted forms of social encounter that were not wholly competitive.'[85] It ought to nurture institutions and forms of life that promote charity. He focuses on the arts: music and drama involve people in a project that is bigger than any individual will; the narrative of competitive individualism is subverted by a group project, a corporate conversation. By this means, 'I may gradually understand the sense in which the robust, primitive, individual self, seeking its fortune in a hostile world and fighting off its competitors, is a naïve fiction. What lies beyond that understanding is a commitment to the charitable conversation that has in fact always and already included me.'[86]

As Williams says later on, he is arguing for a revival of 'civic vitality'. But he immediately acknowledges that this risks seeming to exalt 'social cohesion as an imperative that overrides the protests of a minority voice'.[87] What resists the danger of authoritarianism is 'a recognition that social unity is not ever something unproblematically given or achieved. What I've called civic vitality actually assumes that such cohesion is always in formation: its shape is not yet given and could not be present in any sense without the release, the becoming-audible, of all potential civic voices.'[88] It seems that we need a charity-narrative that resists being reduced to a political ideal, for such would necessarily be factional, violent. Does that mean that it must be 'religious' rather than 'secular'? But if so, that begs further questions – for we have seen that 'religion' tends to contribute to modern alienation.

Basic to contemporary society's problems, Williams explains, is a belief in the 'authentic' inner self. We must instead learn to 'think of selves as being formed in particular histories, particular kinds of interrelations.'[89] The self is formed through social language, and through conversation. Social participation is essential to authentic selfhood – but the social ideal must remain elusive, 'other'; there can be no full and final achievement of social selfhood.

Williams' thesis boils down to a form of Hegelianism that attempts to avoid the key danger of Hegel's vision, the exaltation of the state. The good of each cannot be sought independently of the good of all – but the latter ideal must remain elusive, 'other'.

So how does this relate to the church? A superficial reading of *Lost Icons* would say that of course Williams *really* believes in the church as the true site of the 'social miracle': he is simply choosing to withhold this trump card in this book. But I suggest that his silence on church is more significant. He wants to create a space in which to rethink the business of church away from the conventional categories. As we saw, conventional religious language is charged with deepening the rift between religion and culture, soul and society. This surely extends to ecclesiology. There is a tacit acknowledgement that conventional ecclesiology doesn't work.

The lost icon he does not discuss is the church itself. For surely there is a sense in which the church is in the same position as the monarchy: it cannot do what it theoretically claims to do; it cannot be an effective source of charity. For it is caught up in the culture-wars; it is perceived as being another bid for factional interest (or a weird cluster of such bids). Williams is hinting at something very radical indeed: theology must bypass 'church' in order to communicate the essence of church.

Which is what? It is pan-cultural. Culture as a whole ought to be founded in charity, in the social miracle. He is rejecting a separation between church and world. He is refusing to see secular society as lost; he is expressing anguished love for it. This comes across in the Introduction: 'this is a book attempting to articulate *anger* . . . at a recent history of public corruption and barbarity compounded by apathy and narcissism in our imaginative world.'[90] He is imitating Jesus as he cleanses the temple forecourt, or as he laments the fate of Jerusalem.

The church is not enough. That is the half-hidden message of *Lost Icons*. To celebrate the separate, distinctive society of church is perhaps an evasion of the cultural crisis we inhabit – and of the true scope of Christian hope. The Christian vision must grapple with the regeneration of *all* of society. And to do so it must in a sense forget about church, which so obviously *fails* to mediate charity to society. And it might be unhelpful to sidestep this failure by making supernatural claims for the church as the body of Christ. This might be a strategy of evasion, a means of looking away from society's need for redemption. To present church as a panacea is to devalue contemporary reality, to seek to impose something on it rather than suffer and yearn with it, amidst it.

CHAPTER FOUR

CANTERBURY

E ARLY IN 2002 George Carey announced his resignation: Williams began to be discussed in the press as a potential successor. It was soon clear that he was easily the most popular candidate, despite the opposition of some Evangelicals (seemingly including Carey), who resented his dissenting liberalism on homosexuality. Also, he seemed to advocate disestablishment, and of course he belonged to a church that was already disestablished: this counted against him in some traditionalists' eyes. As did his reputation for political radicalism, highlighted by the mounting international crisis: this was only a few months after September 11. He had criticised the use of military force in Afghanistan the previous November, and as soon as talk of a campaign against Iraq emerged, in the spring of 2002, he took a very strong stance against it. In May he signed a petition declaring that such a war would be 'illegal and immoral'. A reporter asked him whether this stand might be ruining his chances of Canterbury. 'I hope so', he replied. There is a symmetry with his previous appointment to Monmouth: he wanted to be sure that his selectors knew what they were selecting.

But what were they selecting? During the appointment process, there was much discussion of disestablishment – primarily because this process is the clearest reminder of the Crown's involvement in the Church. Some senior churchmen were hinting that Williams' advocacy of disestablishment made him suspect. But his position on that issue was, and is, pretty hard to fathom. He has always been reluctant to show his hand. We have seen him express doubt that establishment is defensible, when the Church will inevitably be seen as unfairly privileged. In 2000 he went further than usual in this direction: 'I believe increasingly that the Church has to earn the right to be heard by the social world . . . Establishment is just one of those things that makes it slightly harder'; he advocated 'disestablishment by a thousand cuts'.[1] In 2002, with Canterbury on the horizon, he toned down his reforming sympathies. He even issued a press release, in response to the re-reporting of his comments of 2000, declaring the issue not to be an immediate concern of the Church – it would need a lot of careful thought 'in the decades to come'. Yet he still reserved the right to sound like a radical on the issue, telling an interviewer that the appointments system needed reform as it sent out 'a message of the subordination of Christianity to some kind of political interest'.[2]

In the summer of 2002 his appointment was confirmed, and his public pronouncements began to be subject to a thousand fine-tooth combs. There was no more hinting at disestablishmentarian designs. The present set-up now seemed on the whole a good thing. 'Establishment,' he told a questioner in September, 'looks like and frequently is a matter of denying vulnerabilities, clinging to privilege; yet some of what establishment has made possible is a sense of the Church as simply there for people in local communities – it has prevented the withdrawal of the Church to middle-class ghettoes.'[3] He subsequently expressed approval for the Christian framework of the coronation service and the 'medieval relationship' between Church and state that it symbolised, and commended 'the whole legacy which gives the Church of England a foot in the door.'[4]

In a television profile, broadcast in December, he sounded like a critic of establishment in a wider sense: 'The Anglican church has bought very deeply into status. It's one of the most ambiguous elements in the whole of that culture – the concern with titles, the concern with little differentiations . . . There's something profoundly anti-Christian in all of that. It's about guarding position, about fencing yourself in. And that's not quite what the Gospel is.'

Questioning the secular

It must be easy enough for such a complex thinker to suppress one aspect of his thought when circumstances make it inconvenient, and foreground another. Circumstances now dictated that he should sound absolutely loyal to the established Church, rather than a critical outsider. In order to keep his sympathy with disestablishment at bay he need only remind himself that he was an influential critic of 'the secular'. This was the theme that he now chose to emphasise. In his first year at Canterbury it dominated his public lectures.

Soon after his appointment was confirmed he delivered the Raymond Williams lecture at the Hay-on-Wye literature festival. The lecture considers the clash of secularism and religion, especially after September 11, and attempts to rethink the relationship between secularism and religious fundamentalism. He defines secularism in terms of 'functionalist' thinking, a failure to see beyond material concerns – and suggests that this is 'the hidden mainspring of certain kinds of modern religiousness'.[5] Religious groups imitate their environment by idolising a single perspective. A vicious circle arises: secularists fear religion, and religion becomes narrower, less authentic. Fundamentalism 'has ceased to give priority to the sense that God's seeing of the world and the self is very strictly incommensurable with any specific human perspective.' It is little surprise that secularism is hostile to such forms of religion.

The challenge is for religions to demonstrate their self-critical capacity. But does this mean moving away from rigid institutional forms? He considers the radical position of the theologian Richard Roberts, who calls for 'a distancing from religious tradition and institution in the name of a looser, more entrepreneurial postmodern religious sensibility.' But this model, says Williams, 'leaves us with insufficient resources for challenging the consumerist assumption that haunts the worlds of new spiritualities . . . The traditional religious institution and the vocabularies of doctrine may be freighted with much moral ambiguity, but they remain carriers of those practices of facing and absorbing disruption without panic that allow imagination to be nourished.' In support of this idea he refers to another recent book, *What is Truth? Towards a Theological Poetics* by Andrew Shanks (a former student of his). He quotes Shanks' argument that 'coherent religious communities' are still needed, to 'preserve a stockpile of potentially resonant religious vocabulary . . . a vocabulary still steeped in prayer.'

Williams' decision for Shanks rather than Roberts is emblematic of his entire ecclesiological thought. Roberts represents the radical-anarchic element in Williams' ecclesiology that we have now traced through twenty-five years, and that it is now more

necessary than ever to repress. A few months earlier he had
reviewed Roberts' book for the *TLS*. For Roberts, he explains, religion must renounce traditional forms and learn 'the skill of the
entrepreneur – perhaps even, in anthropological terms, the "trick-
ster". Only with these skills of adaptation, improvisation, ironic and
carnivalesque engagement in the marketplace will religion work as
"cultural capital" in the way it should.'[6] Williams reacts like a good
responsible conservative, questioning whether there is real account-
ability in the fringe religious activities that Roberts celebrates.
Ought we not to learn the lesson of the 'Nine O'Clock Service'
(an Anglican youth church that drew on rave culture in the early
1990s and ended in mild scandal), he asks: that 'charismatically
dominated religious groups . . . raise the problem of accountable
religious power. Not everyone who becomes involved in such
groups is able to act as a good postmodern consumer, touching
and being touched without being consumed, a *flâneur* of the
transcendent.'[7]

He concludes that the church should *resist* the flow of the
cultural market and prefer 'ethical community' to 'entrepreneurial
bricolage'.[8] But it is pretty obvious that Williams finds Roberts'
vision fascinating, tantalising. He chose to write a broadly sympathetic review of his book, at a time when his work was suddenly
under great scrutiny – and he chose to return to it in a lecture a
few months on. As we shall see, he begins to wonder how something of Roberts' vision can be incorporated into conventional
ecclesiology.

Soon after this Williams also reviewed Shanks' book for the
TLS. For Shanks, theology and the church must be rooted in what
he calls 'shaken' discourse – a pathos of vulnerability and penitence.
The church must 'repent of its love affair with the pathos of glory'.[9]
But this does not lead Shanks in Roberts' direction: questioning the
very defensibility of the institutional church. Instead, in Shanks'
book,

> The Church's vital importance is argued on the grounds that
> there must be a community committed equally to the faithful
> representation of 'shaking' events and to 'conductivity' in
> respect of these events, that is, to making them continuously
> available in rite and narrative. In the tension between these
> poles lies the life-giving energy of the Church, even when that

energy is practically stifled in the institution's neuroses about correctness of thought and action.[10]

Unless it takes the form of a concrete community, Christian tradition will be dissipated, dispersed by the winds of secularism. We must resist the illusion that the secular is 'a space of absence, a benignly untenanted place where citizens can at last relate to each other in innocence of their confessional burdens and prejudices. Secularity is the unreflective world setting its own agenda.' It is a wolf in sheep's clothing; a realm of 'unspoken violence'.[11] Elsewhere, Williams warns of 'modernity' in similar terms. It is 'an atmosphere in which people become increasingly *formless*, cut off from what could give their lives in any given present moment some kind of lasting intelligibility.'[12] Anglicanism 'has the capacity for some far more radical undermining of modernity's unreflective, impatient attitudes than might be expected.'[13] One might object that 'modernity' has liberated millions from poverty and ignorance: why is he intent on seeing modernity as a dirty word? One might also point out that Anglicanism is surely *part* of modernity rather than its antagonist, or its nemesis.

Shortly before Williams was enthroned he gave the annual Dimbleby Lecture. Here he warned of the danger of secular functional arrogance, and called for religious communities to be involved in public life. The modern state, he suggested, no longer provides common culture, or a long-term narrative of national identity. Society is losing sight of the wider picture, the longer view – which religion provides; it 'puts into perspective what my immediate agenda happens to be. And I want to argue that without that relativising moment, our whole politics is likely to be in deep trouble'.[14] Religious tradition offers a larger perspective on life than secular culture provides; it 'makes possible a real questioning of the immediate agenda of a society, the choices that are defined and managed for you by the market.' We need this cultural space more than ever, he suggests. 'The historic role of the Church of England has been and still is making such space available. Its history, its constitutional position – however controversial that may have become for some – means that it is obliged just to be there speaking a certain language, telling a certain story, witnessing to certain non-negotiable things about humanity and about the context in which humanity lives.' It might be, he concludes, that the very

notion of the 'public sphere' relies upon religious vision. For
without traditional communities, and the depth of perspective
they carry, all values will be taken over by the short-termism and
atomism inherent in secularism.

As soon as he is appointed to Canterbury, then, Williams
emphasises the anti-secular dimension of his thought as never
before. This can partly be explained by the new pressure of Church
politics, in particular the reluctance of some Evangelicals to recognise him, on account of his views on homosexuality. Wearing his
anti-secular hat was a way of showing his resistance to liberalism.
Perhaps there is something else at work as well – though this might
seem a speculation too far. Upon assuming leadership of the
Church, perhaps he has to exorcise his own attraction to the secular critique of church, to persuade himself that the church still
needs its traditional structures, for all their ambiguity.

In March 2003 he was enthroned at Canterbury. He spoke of
Jesus as a gift to the world. To mediate that gift is 'the one great purpose of the Church's existence . . . to hold open in its words and
actions a place where we can be with Jesus and be channels for his
free, unanxious, utterly demanding, grown-up love.' This church, he
says, is held together by shared practices rather than a neat system.
The desire for more precise definition should be resisted, 'because
we believe in a Jesus who is truly Lord and God, not the prisoner
of my current thoughts or experiences.' What alone can keep the
church together is confidence that it mediates God's gift to humanity, and gratitude for such a calling. He ends with a significant
little recollection of a visit to an Orthodox monastery. The monk
showing him around pulled a curtain aside to reveal an altar with a
simple picture of Jesus, 'darkened and rather undistinguished':

> But for some reason at that moment it was as if the veil of the
> temple was torn in two: I saw as I had never seen the simple
> fact of Jesus at the heart of all our words and worship, behind
> the curtain of our anxieties and our theories, our struggles and
> our suspicion. Simply there; nothing anyone can do about it,
> there he is as he has promised to be till the world's end.
> Nothing of value happens in the Church that does not start
> from seeing him simply there in our midst, suffering and
> transforming our human disaster.

The church reveals Jesus to the world – this is its 'epiphanic' mission. But this story can also be read somewhat against his intention: the church for the most part allows you to forget what its basic purpose is – it can only reveal Jesus because it first veils him.

Changing church?

Among the commendations that greeted his appointment was one from John Milbank, now teaching in the Unites States. 'Rowan will see no point in "managing decline",' he said. Instead he will seek to alter the cultural image of the church:

> [he] may encourage us to stop thinking simply in terms of 'going to church', but instead in terms of liturgical acts that subversively invade the public space – from obvious things like processions and throwing open church doors to public usage, to less obvious things like challenging the secular dominance of space and time by attempts to introduce more sacramental rhythms.[15]

It would seem that Milbank had this from the horse's mouth. For the second main emphasis of Williams' first year at Canterbury, alongside anti-secularism, was stylistic innovation.

His first presidential address to General Synod in July was overshadowed by the row over homosexual bishops, and the ensuing threat of schism throughout the Anglican Communion. Inevitably, his address begins with reflection on what might keep the Anglican Communion together at such a time. As in his enthronement sermon, he emphasises the prior call of Jesus Christ, his invitation to share in his life. Anglicans must try to recognise each other as sharing a common call. 'Our language, our doctrine, our worship all seek to be effective assurances that we are stepping to the same dance.' Yet, he goes on, there is need for realism about the internal divergence that will follow. He seems to have begun to address the in-fighting over homosexuality, but he now changes the subject almost completely, and discusses innovative forms of worship. There is a need for a 'mixed economy Church' in which the parochial system co-exists with new expressions of church life. This changing of the subject is rather significant: it enacts the very move that he believes the Church must make. It must look away from its internal rows towards fresh opportunities – what can cure it of obsessive arguing over sexuality is a new apprehension of mission. Indeed this change of direction is almost explicit:

At present, we stand at a watershed in the life of the Church of England – not primarily because of the controversies that have been racking us (much as they matter, much as they hurt) but because we have to ask whether we are capable of moving towards a more 'mixed economy' – recognizing church where it appears and having the willingness and the skill to work with it.

These 'new ways of being church' include church plants, evening meetings, hymns in the pub, informal networks, Christian music festivals. 'This is where the unexpected growth happens, where the unlikely contacts are often made; where the Church is renewed (as it so often is) from the edges, not the centre.' The Church must work hard not to lose touch with these movements:

> That's to say we need ordained leadership which is capable of making and servicing connections between lots of different styles of 'church' – leadership which is therefore very clear about theological priorities, not protective of its status, skilled in listening and interpreting what may seem very different language groups to each other. That's why, incidentally, when I've been asked about my priorities as Archbishop, I have regularly mentioned both the encouragement of new styles of church and the need for theological education.

As we saw, the previous summer Williams was expressing grave reservations about Richard Roberts' vision of a deregulated religious market. Yet he now expresses a desire to see something similar occur *within* the Church. To borrow a public-policy analogy, he wants to introduce an internal market to the Church of England, in which radical new forms are kept within the fold of the institution.

Early the following year a new Church report on the subject appeared: *Mission-Shaped Church*. In his foreword Williams wrote that the present challenge 'is not to force everything into the familiar mould; but neither is it to tear up the rulebook and start from scratch (as if that were ever possible or realistic).'[16] There is scope for diversity within the institution, 'so long as we have ways of identifying the same living Christ at the heart of every expression of Christian life in common. This immediately raises large questions about how different churches keep in contact with each other, and about the kinds of leadership we need for this to happen.'[17] When the report was debated at Synod in February 2004, Williams restated his enthusiasm, declaring that we 'stand at something of a kairos moment' – and significantly, he reaffirmed the role of the bishop in mission, as the force that keeps innovative impulses under ecclesiastical supervision.

In May he delivered a lecture on the challenges facing new Anglican priests. The underlying challenge is to move away from a view of the church as 'essentially a lot of people who have something in common called Christian faith and get together to share it with each other and to communicate it to other people "outside".'[18] Instead, the church is 'a place where we can see clearly – God, God's creation, ourselves. It is a place or dimension in the universe that is in some way growing towards being the universe itself in restored relation to God.' He hopes his comments will make sense 'in the new styles of church life towards which we are undoubtedly moving':

> An ordained ministry that reminds the Church what it is in terms of its invitation into Christ's place will be an essential aspect of that necessary renewal which takes us beyond the identification of 'Church' with the way we have historically run things. Ironically in the eyes of some, a theology for 'emerging church' ought to underline the rationale for ordained ministry, Catholic ministry, not to obscure it; because an emerging church without the recognizable signs and relations embodied in Catholic ministry is in serious danger of lapsing into the mode of a human assembly of those who agree and sympathise with each other.

This is essentially the same point he was making 20 years back: to be catholic (aspiring to universality, capable of adapting to new situations), the church must be Catholic (ballasted by its traditional hierarchical structure). In the same month he gave a newspaper interview in which he restated the challenge:

> How do we find the kind of structural flexibility that . . . responds effectively and fairly promptly to the new expressions of Church that are around . . .? It's got to be a Church which can travel fairly lightly in terms of its structures and respond quite flexibly to where its new needs arise. I'd like to be judged on how far I've enabled that to happen.[19]

It is a bold vision: reinvigorating the Church of England, pointing it beyond its ancient feuding to its true task of unveiling the new humanity. It is especially bold in the light of what we have seen: his anguished acknowledgement that ecclesiology is marked by the most extreme and unavoidable crisis.

CONCLUSION

THIS BOOK HAS SOUGHT to highlight a tension in Williams' thought between two powerful theological impulses. The first is postmodern (meaning above all 'cultural-linguistic') Catholicism: the actual practices of the church are the outward essence of this religion. The other, less officially acknowledged, impulse is eschato-logical universalism: the truth of this tradition lies in its heralding of a new unlimited human community:

> In short, the question of Jesus' status arises out of his role in the formation of a human community different from what we ordinarily think of as 'natural' communities, a community whose limits are at the same time the ultimate natural 'limits' – 'the ends of the earth'. *The world we inhabit* is the potential scope of the community that is created by relation to Jesus. It is, you might say, a social vision that shapes the doctrine of the Incarnation, in the first instance, not the reverse; or rather, it is the social *fact* of a community with no foreordained boundaries.[1]

This illustrates both sides. For he presents the Gospel as the call to a universal human society – and then in the second half of the last sentence he roots this vision in the church. The vision is a fact, a concrete reality whose name is church. Can one have it both ways?

Let no one pretend that there is no contradiction. The vision of unrestricted human society is necessarily at odds with any actual institution. An institution will always grow political roots, and will always define itself, limit itself, police its boundaries. And the Christian movement is a movement *away* from such limits.

Theology trains itself not to see a contradiction here, but there is one. (Williams, perhaps, trains himself both to see it and not to see it.)

This is the central problem of Williams' theology, the one he returns to in almost everything he writes. Every institutional church not only expresses the Christian vision, but also obscures and distorts it. Every institutional church not only serves Christ, but, in one of his most vivid phrases, 'deserves to be broken on the rock of Christ'. Or, to cite another vivid phrase, the church is meant to be 'in love with the kingdom', but in reality it is otherwise: to call it a 'love-hate' relationship would be overstating it, for the church generally seems to have forgotten about the Kingdom altogether.

Given the monumental failure of church, why persist in defending it so loyally? There is for Williams a one-word answer to this: the Eucharist. As we put it earlier on, the key to his ecclesiology is the fact that he really believes in the Eucharist. The ritual representation of Jesus' passion and resurrection is the engine of the Christian vision: this ritual is utopian, in the sense that it offers a glimpse of a healed world – and a first step towards it (a first step that is always the only possible step). And at the same time the Eucharist is the justification of the cultural burden we call church. The church 'is first and foremost the epiphany of God's action in the paschal events'.[2] Because there must be Eucharist, there must be church. Without the Eucharist, Christianity is abstract idealism, prey to every passing fashion. Riteless it's rootless. Because it has the Eucharist at its heart, the church can be forgiven – for turning the vision of total peace into something all too human. Williams' agenda as a theologian and a bishop is to put the spotlight on Christianity's central rite, to let it speak. The fact that the church stages this primal rite about Jesus is what justifies it.

But *does* this justify the church? For surely it does not remove the core problem: that the ideal of a truly universal human society is contradicted by the very existence of the church as a coherent, self-regarding institution (which even a 'eucharistic' church remains). A culturally substantial church stands in the way of its own vision. It betrays, as it expresses, the Kingdom of God. Or rather, it expresses the Kingdom of God as something inevitably betrayed, as impossible – and it offers *itself* as the compensation, the replacement, the more realistic version of the ideal. My argument with Williams is that he perceives this questionable dynamic at the heart of church but learns to live with it. He backs off, affirming with great eloquence the adequacy of conventional ecclesiology. In a sense (I am afraid this will sound very sacrilegious to orthodox ears), his faith in the Eucharist is what holds his theology back. His articulation of the social vision that is Christianity, the Kingdom of God, is over-determined by his attachment to the Kingdom's ambiguous ritual representation (ambiguous because necessarily staged by an institution that defers the Kingdom).

In the year that Williams began studying theology, Donald MacKinnon gave a lecture in which he echoed Bonhoeffer's call for a new spirit of theological audacity:

> Theological progress may be dependent upon the criticism of the Church's institutional experience, even the rejection of long tracts of that experience as fundamentally invalid. In such criticism may well lie the necessary condition of really fundamental theological progress . . . the sort of renewal the present not only demands but seems to make possible.[3]

We must beware of fundamentalism in a wide sense, he insists: 'ecclesiological and liturgical' forms are 'as deadly in their way as the more familiar biblical variant'. Throughout his career Williams has certainly been conscious of this warning, but he has not let it distract him from his fundamental ecclesiological conservatism. His theological vision is consciously limited: it glimpses new possibilities that it refrains from pursuing, preferring to shelter in the sturdy ruins of Christendom. It is haunted by the option it refuses, the radicalism it renounces, the road not taken.

NOTES

Prologue: Show Business

1. Eric Gill, *Autobiography* (Lund Humphries, London, 1992), pp. 71–2.
2. Ibid., p. 186.
3. Ibid., pp. 186, 171.

Introduction

1. In what follows, I will generally use 'church', except when referring to a particular institution, e.g. 'the Roman Catholic Church'. Like most theologians, Williams prefers 'Church' in almost all cases. My use of the lower case has a corrective intention, as will become clear.

1. Some Background

1. Interview with Charles Moore, *Daily Telegraph*, 12 February 2003.
2. Ibid.
3. Rowan Williams, 'Atonement', lectures delivered to Bristol Church Union, 3 September 2002 (from tape recording, unpublished).
4. Interview with Roland Ashby, *The Melbourne Anglican*, June 2002 (online).
5. Interview with Geoff Robson, *Anglican Media Sydney*, 27 May 2002 (online).
6. Rupert Shortt, *Rowan Williams, an Introduction* (DLT, 2003), p. 25.
7. Interview with Charles Moore, *Daily Telegraph*, 12 February 2003.
8. John Henry Newman, *Apologia Pro Vita Sua* (Fontana, London, 1959), p. 132.
9. Ibid., p. 133.
10. Kenneth Leech, 'Some Light from the Noel Archives', in Leech, ed., *Conrad Noel and the Catholic Crusade: a critical evaluation* (Jubilee Group, 1993), p. 49.
11. Ibid., p. 47.
12. Rowan Williams, '*Honest to God* and the 1960s' (2002), in Williams, *Anglican Identities* (DLT, 2004), p. 109.
13. Rowan Williams, 'Michael Ramsey', in Williams, *Open to Judgement: Sermons and Addresses* (DLT, London, 1993), p. 224.
14. Michael Ramsey, quoted in Adrian Hastings, *A History of English Christianity: 1920–2000* (SCM, London, 2001), p. 533.

15. Rowan Williams, 'Honest to God and the 1960s' (2002), in Williams, Anglican Identities, op. cit.

16. Rowan Williams, 'B. F. Westcott: the Fate of Liberal Anglicanism' (2001), in Williams, Anglican Identities, op. cit., pp. 85–6.

17. Rowan Williams, 'Analysing Atheism: Unbelief and the World of Faiths', a lecture delivered at Georgetown University, 29 March 2004 (online).

18. Fergus Kerr, editorial, New Blackfriars (Blackwell), May 2004.

19. Inaugural lecture at Cambridge, 1969, in A. N. Wilson, Iris Murdoch, As I Knew Her (Hutchinson, London, 2003), p. 177.

20. Donald MacKinnon quoted in Richard Roberts, 'Theological Rhetoric and Moral Passion in MacKinnon's "Barth"' (1987), in Roberts, A Theology on its Way? (T. & T. Clark, Edinburgh, 1991), p. 162.

21. Ibid., p. 168.

22. Donald MacKinnon, Themes in Theology (T. & T. Clark, Edinburgh 1987), p. 4.

23. Donald MacKinnon, 'Kenosis and Establishment', in The Stripping of the Altars, the Gore Memorial Lecture delivered in Westminster Abbey, and other papers and essays on related topics (Fontana, London, 1969).

24. Rowan Williams, 'Trinity and Ontology', in On Christian Theology (Blackwell, 1999), p. 162.

25. Rowan Williams, 'Eastern Orthodox Theology', in David Ford, ed., The Modern Theologians (Blackwell, 1997), p. 154.

26. Rowan Williams, Sergeii Bulgakov: Towards a Russian Political Theology (T. & T. Clark, Edinburgh, 1999), p. 233.

27. Rowan Williams, 'Eastern Orthodox Theology', in Ford, The Modern Theologians, op. cit., p. 163.

28. Rowan Williams, Obituary of Florovsky, Sobornost 1980, vol. 2, no. 1, p. 72.

29. Rowan Williams, 'Eastern Orthodox Theology', in Ford, The Modern Theologians, op. cit., p. 155.

30. Interview with David S. Cunningham, Christian Century, 24 April 2002 (online).

31. Timothy Ware, The Orthodox Church (Penguin, 1963), pp. 155–6.

32. Roland Ashby, 'Quarrying for God' (interview with Williams), The Melbourne Anglican, March 1999.

33. Ibid.

34. Bernard Begonzi, 'The English Catholics', Encounter, January 1965, p. 30.

35. Interview with David S. Cunningham, Christian Century, 24 April 2002 (online).

36. Hans Urs Von Balthasar, Engagement with God, p. 41.

37. Ibid., p. 42.

38. Ibid., pp. 99–100.

39. Thomas Merton, The Seven Storied Mountain (Sheldon Press, London, 1975), p. 65.

40. Ibid., pp. 65–6.

41. David Jones, 'A Christmas Message 1960', in Jones, The Dying Gaul and Other Writings (Faber & Faber, London, 1978), p. 167.

42. Ibid., p. 171.

43. Rowan Williams, 'Eric Gill', Sobornost, vol. 7, no. 4, 1977, p. 264.

44. Rowan Williams, 'Poetic and Religious Imagination', *Theology*, vol. 80, 1977, p. 185.
45. Rowan Williams, 'Liberation Theology and the Anglican Tradition', in David Nicholls and Rowan Williams, *Politics and Theological Identity: Two Anglican Essays* (Jubilee Group, 1984), p. 10.
46. Ibid., p. 11.
47. Rowan Williams, 'Violence and the Gospel in South Africa', *New Blackfriars*, 1984, p. 505.
48. Ludwig Wittgenstein, in Rush Rhees, ed., *Reflections of Wittgenstein* (Oxford University Press, 1981), p. 114.

2. Oxbridge
1. Rowan Williams, 'Atonement', lectures delivered to Bristol Church Union, 3 September 2002 (from tape recording, unpublished).
2. Ibid.
3. Rowan Williams, 'To Give and Not to Count the Cost, a sermon preached at Mirfield in February 1976', *Sobornost*, Summer 1977, series 7, no. 5, p. 403.
4. Interview with Charles Moore, *Daily Telegraph*, 12 February 2003.
5. Rowan Williams, '*Honest to God* and the 1960s' (2002), in Williams, *Anglican Identities* (DLT, 2004), pp. 114–15.
6. Rowan Williams, 'Liberation Theology and the Anglican Tradition', in David Nicholls and Rowan Williams, *Politics and Theological Identity: Two Anglican Essays* (Jubilee Group, 1984), p. 6.
7. Ibid., p. 22.
8. Ibid., p. 17.
9. Ibid., p. 18.
10. Ibid., p. 22.
11. Rowan Williams, 'Incarnation and the Renewal of Community', in *On Christian Theology* (Blackwell, 1999), p. 234.
12. Rowan Williams, *The Wound of Knowledge* (DLT, 1979), p. 1.
13. Ibid., p. 2.
14. Ibid., p. 7.
15. Ibid., p. 181.
16. Ibid., p. 94.
17. Benedict Green, quoted in Rupert Shortt, *Rowan Williams, an Introduction* (DLT, 2003), p. 32.
18. Mark Santer, ed., *Their Lord and Ours: Approaches to Authority, Community and the Unity of the Church* (SPCK, London, 1982), p. 93.
19. Ibid.
20. Ibid., p. 94.
21. Ibid., p. 95.
22. Ibid., p. 96–7.
23. Ibid., p. 99.
24. Ibid., p. 100.
25. Ibid., p. 106.
26. Ibid., p. 108.
27. Ibid.

28. Ibid., p. 109.
29. Ibid.
30. Ibid., pp. 109–10.
31. Rowan Williams, 'The Necessary Non-Existence of God', in *Simone Weil's Philosophy of Culture: Readings toward a Divine Humanity*, ed. by Richard H. Bell (Cambridge University Press, 1993), p. 54.
32. Rowan Williams, *Resurrection* (DLT), p. 3.
33. Ibid., p. 4.
34. Ibid., p. 63.
35. Ibid., p. 43.
36. Ibid., p. 49.
37. Ibid.
38. Ibid., p. 54.
39. ibid., p. 58.
40. Ibid., p. 63–4.
41. Ibid., p. 64.
42. Ibid., p. 71.
43. Rowan Williams, *The Truce of God* (Fount Original, London, 1982), p. 29.
44. Ibid., pp. 33–4.
45. Ibid., pp. 31–2.
46. Ibid., pp. 113–14.
47. Rowan Williams, 'Eucharistic Sacrifice – the Roots of Metaphor', Grove Liturgical Study No. 31, 1982, p. 32.
48. Rowan Williams, 'What is Catholic Orthodoxy?', in Leech and Williams, eds, *Essays Catholic and Radical*, pp. 20–21.
49. Ibid., p. 23.
50. Ibid., p. 24.
51. Rowan Williams, '"Religious Realism": On Not Quite Agreeing with Don Cupitt', *Modern Theology*, 1985, p. 17.
52. Ibid., p. 20.
53. Ibid., p. 21.
54. Rowan Williams, 'The Suspicion of Suspicion: Wittgenstein and Bonhoeffer', in Richard H. Bell, ed., *The Grammar of the Heart: Thinking with Kierkegaard and Wittgenstein* (Harper and Row, San Francisco, 1988), p. 36.
55. Rowan Williams and James Atkinson, 'On Doing Theology' in *Stepping Stones: Joint Essays on Anglican Catholic and Evangelical Unity*, ed. by Christina Baxter et al. (Hodder & Stoughton, 1987), p. 4.
56. Rowan Williams, 'Trinity and Revelation' in *On Christian Theology* (Blackwell, 1999), pp. 143–4.
57. Ibid.
58. Rowan Williams, 'The Nature of a Sacrament' in *On Christian Theology*, op. cit., p. 202.
59. Ibid., p. 203.
60. Ibid.
61. Ibid., pp. 204–5.
62. Ibid., p. 205.
63. Ibid., p. 206.

64. Rowan Williams, *Arius: Heresy and Tradition* (DLT, 1987), p. 23.

65. Ibid., p. 25.

66. Ibid., p. 239.

67. Ibid., p. 244.

68. Rowan Williams, 'Does it make sense to speak of pre-Nicene orthodoxy?' in Williams, ed., *The Making of Orthodoxy; Essays in Honour of Henry Chadwick* (CUP, 1989), p. 3.

69. Ibid., p. 10.

70. Ibid., pp. 16–17.

71. Rowan Williams, 'Nobody Knows Who I am Till Judgement Morning', in *On Christian Theology*, op. cit., pp. 287–8.

72. Rowan Williams, 'Incarnation and the Renewal of Community', in *On Christian Theology*, op. cit., p. 226.

73. Ibid., p. 228.

74. Ibid., pp. 230–31.

75. Ibid., pp. 231–2.

76. Ibid., pp. 233–4.

77. Ibid.

78. Rowan Williams, 'The Judgement of the World', in *On Christian Theology*, op. cit., pp. 36–7.

79. Rowan Williams, 'Trinity and Pluralism', in *On Christian Theology*, op. cit., p. 179.

80. Rowan Williams, 'The Finality of Christ', in *On Christian Theology*, op. cit., p. 100.

3. Wales

1. Rowan Williams, Prologue to *On Christian Theology* (Blackwell, 1999), p. xiii.

2. Interview with Geoff Robson, *Anglican Media Sydney*, 27 May 2002 (online).

3. Interview with Roy Hattersley, *Observer*, 11 July 2004.

4. Report on evangelism to Lambeth Conference, 1998.

5. Rowan Williams, *Teresa of Avila* (DLT, 1991), p. 170.

6. Ibid., p. 171.

7. Rowan Williams, 'Catholic and Reformed', July 1993, accessible on the Affirming Catholicism website.

8. Rowan Williams, 'The Future of the Papacy – An Anglican View' (1997), unpublished.

9. Rowan Williams, 'Is there a Christian Sexual Ethic?', in Williams, *Open to Judgement: Sermons and Addresses* (DLT, London, 1994), p. 164.

10. Ibid., p. 167.

11. Rowan Williams, 'Talk of the Devil', in Jeffrey John, ed., *Living Evangelism: Affirming Catholicism and Sharing the Faith* (DLT, London, 1996), p. 101.

12. Rowan Williams, 'Interiority and Epiphany: a Reading in New Testament Ethics', in *On Christian Theology*, op. cit., pp. 256, 258.

13. George Carey, *Know the Truth, a Memoir* (HarperCollins, 2004), p. 298.

14. Rowan Williams, 'Politics and the Soul: a reading of the City of God', in *Milltown Studies* (no. 19/20, Dublin, 1987), pp. 55–72, 58.

15. Ibid., p. 62.

16. Ibid., p. 58.
17. Rowan Williams, 'Christianity and the Ideal of Detachment', 1988 Frank Lake Memorial Lecture (Oxford, 1989), p. 9.
18. Rowan Williams, John Mere's Commemoration Sermon, St Benet's Church, Cambridge, 20 April 2004.
19. Rowan Williams, 'Violence, Society and the Sacred', lecture delivered at St Antony's College Oxford, 26 October 1989, Oxford Project for Peace Studies, Paper no. 18, p. 7.
20. Ibid., p. 9.
21. Ibid., p. 10.
22. Ibid., p. 11.
23. Rowan Williams, 'Challenge of Brotherhood', review of *Faith Beyond Resentment: fragments catholic and Gay* by James Alison, *The Tablet*, 2 June 2001.
24. Rowan Williams, John Mere's Commemoration Sermon, St Benet's Church, Cambridge, 20 April 2004.
25. Rowan Williams, 'Christian Resources for the Renewal of Vision', in *The Renewal of Social Vision*, ed. by Alison J. Elliot and Ian Swanson (Centre for Theology and Public Issues, Edinburgh, 1989), p. 3.
26. Ibid., p. 4.
27. Ibid., p. 5.
28. Ibid.
29. Ibid.
30. Ibid., pp. 6–7.
31. George Lindbeck, *The Nature of Doctrine: Religion and Theology in a Postliberal Age* (SPCK, London, 1984), p. 34.
32. Rowan Williams, 'The Judgement of the World', in *On Christian Theology*, op. cit., p. 31.
33. Ibid.
34. Ibid., p. 38.
35. Ibid., p. 40.
36. Ibid., p. 380.
37. Ibid., p. 6.
38. Rowan Williams, 'Saving Time: Thoughts on Practice, Patience and Vision', *New Blackfriars*, 1992, p. 319.
39. Ibid.
40. Ibid., p. 321.
41. Ibid.
42. Ibid.
43. Ibid., p. 322.
44. Ibid., p. 323.
45. Ibid.
46. Interview with David S. Cunningham, *Christian Century*, 24 April 2002.
47. Jacques Derrida, quoted in Kevin Hart, 'The God Effect', in Philip Blond, ed., *Postsecular Philosophy* (Routledge, London, 1998), p. 262.
48. Rowan Williams, 'Hegel and the Gods of Postmodernity', in Phillipa Berry and Andrew Wernick, eds, *Shadow of Spirit* (Routledge, 1992), p. 77.
49. Ibid.

50. Rowan Williams, 'Between Politics and Metaphysics: Reflections in the Wake of Gillian Rose', *Modern Theology* 11:1, January 1995, p. 19.

51. Rowan Williams, 'Mission and Christology', J. C. Jones Memorial Lecture (Church Missionary Society, Welsh Members' Council, 1994), pp. 4–5.

52. Ibid., p. 6.

53. Ibid., p. 7.

54. Ibid. p. 12.

55. Ibid., p. 13.

56. Ibid., p. 21.

57. Rowan Williams, 'Between the Cherubim: The Empty Tomb and the Empty Throne' (1996), in *On Christian Theology*, op. cit., p. 193.

58. Rowan Williams, 'Doing the Works of God', in Williams, *Open to Judgement: Sermons and Addresses* (DLT, London, 1993), p. 256.

59. Ibid., p. 258.

60. Ibid., p. 259.

61. Ibid., p. 263.

62. Ibid., p. 277.

63. Rowan Williams, 'Logic and Spirit in Hegel', in Philip Blond, ed., *Postsecular Philosophy* (Routledge, London, 1998), p. 262.

64. Ibid., p. 128.

65. Rowan Williams, 'Theology and the Churches' (1995), in Williams, *Anglican Identities* (DLT, 2004), pp. 91–2.

66. Ibid., pp. 97–8.

67. Ibid., p. 98.

68. Ibid., p. 99.

69. Ibid., pp. 99–100.

70. Ibid., p. 102.

71. Rowan Williams, Preface to *God and Reality: Essays on Christian Non-Realism*, ed. by Colin Crowder (1997), p. vii.

72. Ibid., p. ix.

73. Rowan Williams, 'No Joy, No Terror, No Tears', *Church Times*, 17 July 1998.

74. Rowan Williams, 'Fully Human: review of *Jesus, the Teacher Within* by Lawrence Freeman', *The Tablet*, 2 June 2001.

75. Rowan Williams, *Lost Icons: reflections on cultural bereavement* (Continuum, T. & T. Clark, Edinburgh, 2000), p. 4.

76. Ibid., p. 7.

77. Ibid., p. 54.

78. Ibid., p. 55.

79. Ibid., p. 62.

80. Ibid., p. 71.

81. Ibid., p. 63.

82. Ibid., p. 64.

83. Ibid., p. 66.

84. Ibid., p. 60.

85. Ibid., p. 86.

86. Ibid., p. 93.

87. Ibid., p. 116.

88. Ibid., p. 116.
89. Ibid., p. 112.
90. Ibid., p. 9.

4. Canterbury

1. Speaking at the Greenbelt festival, August 2000.
2. Interview with Graham Turner, *Daily Telegraph*, 24 July 2002.
3. Rowan Williams, Lecture on Atonement, Bristol, 3 September 2002, unpublished.
4. For further material on this issue see my *Against Establishment, an Anglican Polemic* (DLT, 2003), pp. 124–30.
5. Rowan Williams, Raymond Williams Lecture at Hay-on-Wye Festival, July 2002 (online).
6. Rowan Williams, 'Against the Market?', review of Richard H. Roberts, *Religion, Theology and the Human Sciences* (*TLS*, 29 March 2002), p. 4.
7. Ibid.
8. Ibid.
9. Rowan Williams, 'What Shakes Us', review of Andrew Shanks, *What is Truth?: Towards a Theological Poetics*, and Stanley Hauerwas, *With the Grain of the Universe: the Church's Witness and Natural Theology* (*TLS*, 4 July 2003), p. 10.
10. Ibid.
11. Ibid.
12. Rowan Williams, Preface to *Anglicanism: the Answer to Modernity*, ed. by Duncan Dormor et al. (Continuum, 2003), p. vii.
13. Ibid., p. x.
14. Rowan Williams, the Richard Dimbleby Lecture 2002, Westminster School, London, 19 December 2002.
15. John Milbank, Editorial, *Religion and Ethics Newsweekly*, 26 July 2002.
16. Rowan Williams, Foreword to *Mission-Shaped Church*, ed. by Graham Cray (Church House, 2004), p. vii.
17. Ibid.
18. Rowan Williams, 'The Christian Priest Today', lecture on the occasion of the 150th anniversary of Ripon College, Cuddesdon, 28 May 2004.
19. Interview with Mary Ann Sieghart, *The Times*, 26 May 2004.

Conclusion

1. Rowan Willliams, *On Christian Theology* (Blackwell, 1999) pp. 231–2.
2. Ibid., pp. 92–3.
3. Donald MacKinnon, 'Kenosis and Establishment', in *The Stripping of the Altars, the Gore Memorial Lecture delivered in Westminster Abbey, and other papers and essays on related topics* (Fontana, London, 1969), pp. 18–19.